OPPORTUN

in

Biotechnology Careers

OPPORTUNITIES

in

Biotechnology
Careers

REVISED EDITION

SHELDON S. BROWN

New York Chicago San Francisco Lisbon London Madrid Mexico City
Milan New Delhi San Juan Seoul Singapore Sydney Toronto

The *McGraw-Hill* Companies

Library of Congress Cataloging-in-Publication Data

Brown, Sheldon S., 1937–
    Opportunities in biotechnology careers / Sheldon S. Brown. —Rev. ed.
        p.   cm.
    Includes bibliographical references.
    ISBN 0-07-147605-9 (alk. paper)
    I. Title.

    TP248.215. B766   2007
    660.6023—dc22

                                                              2006028898

Copyright © 2007 by The McGraw-Hill Companies, Inc. All rights reserved. Printed in the United States of America. Except as permitted under the United States Copyright Act of 1976, no part of this publication may be reproduced or distributed in any form or by any means, or stored in a database or retrieval system, without the prior written permission of the publisher.

1 2 3 4 5 6 7 8 9 10 11 12 13 14 15 16 17 18 19   DOC/DOC   1 0 9 8 7

ISBN-13: 978-0-07-147605-8
ISBN-10:   0-07-147605-9

Interior design by Rattray Design

McGraw-Hill books are available at special quantity discounts to use as premiums and sales promotions, or for use in corporate training programs. For more information, please write to the Director of Special Sales, Professional Publishing, McGraw-Hill, Two Penn Plaza, New York, NY 10121-2298. Or contact your local bookstore.

This book is printed on acid-free paper.

In loving memory of my parents, Rabbi Jacob M. Brown and Tillie Brown. I would be blessed if I could possess a fraction of their kindness, wisdom, and courage!

Contents

infections every day. Other medical frontiers.
Advances in diagnosis. Scope of biomedical advances.

What research biologists do. Job titles and
descriptions. Scientific jobs outside of product
research and development. Daily activities in the lab.
Jobs in research organizations and corporations.
Nonscientific biotechnology careers.

Majors and interdisciplinary emphases in
biotechnology. Growth and changes in biotechnology
education. Associate degree programs. Bachelor's and
graduate-level programs. Curriculum examples.
Research centers. Continuing education. Staying
informed.

Industry facts and trends. Current employment.
Biopharmaceutical outlook. Agricultural outlook. Sales
and revenues. Employment and income. Changing
personnel needs.

Communicating. Cooperating. Making the most of
experience. Coping with frustrations. Being sensitive
to public perceptions. Thinking creatively.

7. Finding the Right Job   **109**

Getting started. Internet job search sites. Researching
corporations. Learning from the associations.
Conferences, conventions, and career fairs.
Networking. Temporary and contract work. Cover
letters and résumés. Succeeding at interviews.
Working with recruiters. Choosing well in an
expanding field.

FOREWORD

IN THE JARGON of the age, some people are predicting that when future generations look back they will refer to the twentieth century as the Computer Age and the twenty-first century as the Age of Life Sciences—or the Bio-Century. As we watch the scope of the true revolution in life sciences that is occurring all around us, and we see more every day how it is affecting the lives of people and our environment in all parts of the world, I suspect that this prediction may prove to be accurate.

The era we live in is being made more exciting because of the enormous unfolding of potential in biotechnology and related sciences. Indeed, in recent years, biotechnology—"where scientists use living things to achieve practical purposes"—has produced startling headlines and captured the imaginations of people around the world. Achievements such as identifying the precise locations and composition of the more than thirty thousand genes in the human body, completed in 2003, and the ongoing discovery of new secrets about DNA continually put biotechnology in the spotlight.

Application of the ever-expanding body of knowledge in the field of biotechnology has already brought about revolutionary changes in human and animal health care, agriculture, and energy production. What once was a field anchored primarily in research but with relatively few practical applications, now is making an enormous impact on our lives. In preventing and treating diseases, in improving agricultural crops, and in finding new ways to produce energy with far less pollution, practical applications in biotechnology have become almost commonplace. We receive the news in newspaper headlines, on television and radio, and on the Internet every day. Indeed, whole new related industries have been born— one of which is reporting the biotechnology news.

With the increasing importance of biotechnology, more and more companies, research organizations, and other employers depend upon the work of highly trained professionals to conduct research and to perform a variety of other important functions. This means that career opportunities are and will continue to be plentiful for those with the right skills and education. It means, too, that if you love science and have imagination and the desire to create, there may be opportunity for you in this field.

Imagine using principles of biotechnology to develop a new medicine or vaccine for a previously incurable disease. Or think about making fruits and vegetables more nutritious, longer lasting, and more resistant to insects and disease by applying the knowledge and skills of this fascinating science. Perhaps you might serve on a team that cleans up a hazardous waste site and turns it into safe, productive land; or you might conduct research on the new frontiers of molecular biology or gene therapy. Professionals who work in biotechnology will literally create our future.

Pursuing a career in biotechnology requires hard work and dedication, and it also offers significant rewards. The chance to do challenging work that can actually help to improve the human condition holds the promise for a noble career.

Opportunities in Biotechnology Careers provides an overview of this field and the kinds of jobs that exist, and describes how to prepare for them. It also shows you how to continue to learn about the biotechnology field in depth and how to keep up to date and informed as you build your professional career.

If an occupation in this area sounds appealing, please read on. Who knows? Perhaps a career in the exciting field of biotechnology awaits you in the very near future.

James C. Greenwood
President and CEO
Biotechnology Industry Organization

Acknowledgments

THE AUTHOR DEEPLY appreciates all the individuals and organizations that contributed to this book, including the following: the B.C. Biotechnology Alliance; the Biotechnology Industry Organization; Dr. Mark Bloom; Daniel and Sharon Brown; Charlene J. Coursen; Lisa Idry; David Jensen; Marina Kney; Sarah Manning; the Massachusetts Biotechnology Council; the Montgomery County High Technology Council, Inc.; the North Carolina Biotechnology Center; Susan Saraquse; and Dr. David Smith.

The author also wishes to thank Barbara Wood Donner for her assistance in writing the revision for the current edition.

INTRODUCTION

ONLY A FEW decades ago, people with training in the life sciences typically pursued careers in agriculture, biology, medicine, or academia, with few other options. Until only recently, biotechnology could hardly be called a field or an industry at all.

In recent years, however, a number of factors, including new technology spearheaded by the computer revolution; major new needs created by global population growth, poverty, and wars; climate change; serious diseases such as HIV/AIDS and avian flu; and major international economic financial opportunities and pressures have combined to cause an unprecedented growth spurt that appears likely to continue into the foreseeable future. Today, with thousands of new biotechnology companies and government and academic programs, there are innumerable career options, scientific and nonscientific, for anyone interested in the life sciences.

Because of financial and governmental pressures of recent years, many American biotechnology firms have shifted their focus from research and development (R&D) to producing and selling marketable products. Many other new companies have been started up in the last ten to twenty years to operate in this part of the field, as well. Financial and legal firms specializing in biotechnology are proliferating. Although careers in biotechnology have traditionally required scientific backgrounds, this industry shift has opened up a wider range of job opportunities by creating a greater demand for people with expertise in nonscientific areas, including business and financial managers, communications and marketing personnel, salespeople, lawyers, regulatory specialists, and financial analysts. Scientists such as engineers and computer scientists, with backgrounds outside the life sciences, are finding increasing numbers of jobs in biotechnology as well.

Critical challenges exist for biotechnology today. Financial resources in some parts of the world cannot support the work that needs to be done. In other areas, finances are going to the more-profitable instead of the more-needed areas. Political, social, and religious controversy inhibits research in many areas, in some cases, where needs for advancement are greatest. Global warming, increasing poverty with its accompanying hunger and disease, increasing pressures of food, water, and fuel shortages, the threat of new diseases, and other world crises cry out for solutions, and part of these will come from biotechnology. The world needs some miracles both now and in the decades ahead.

Biotechnology has already profoundly changed the quality of our lives through improved medicine, diagnostics, agriculture, and waste management, to name a few of the many areas of accomplishments by this burgeoning industry. Because the field is growing fast, there are unique opportunities to forge new territory, make new discoveries, and introduce useful innovations into the marketplace. A career in biotechnology offers exciting opportunities today for anyone motivated to seek out and acquire the necessary education, training, and experience. Perhaps this book will help you determine if and how you might fit into the challenging and continually transforming world of the science and industry of biotechnology.

1

Overview of the Biotechnology Field

Biotechnology in the twenty-first century is not your grand-parents' biotechnology! In the 1930s and 1940s, biotechnology was making some of its biggest headlines with a new drug called an *antibiotic*—the "Miracle Drug" penicillin—and with the lifesaving use of blood "plasma" by medics in helping the armed forces in World War II. In the 1940s, in agriculture, seed companies were making big news with new breeds of corn that they were calling *hybrids*.

From Golden Corn to Golden Rice

Driving around the highways and country roads of America in the mid-twentieth century, you could see big pictures of giant ears of golden corn painted on billboards and on the sides of wooden barns advertising the new hybrid seed varieties. There was a lot of controversy. Farmers were unsure that the crops would be safe for their livestock to eat. Consumers were cautious, too, and the new crop prices were uncertain, but the hybrid breeds were bigger, plumper, hardier, and, in many ways, just plain better. Soon, despite the controversy, to be able to compete successfully, even small farmers began to take up the new varieties of seeds.

Gradually the controversy over hybrid corn subsided. However, the germination of biotechnology as an industry was almost silently but vibrantly sprouting and spreading out, growing in just a couple of decades from a few dozen small research labs in a handful of countries to hundreds of complex high-technology labs worldwide. Today the industry is bursting through countless new frontiers across America and is operating in nearly every country of the world.

One of the most famous examples of the strides of biotechnology in recent years, and one of the most far-reaching in its effects, is that of Golden Rice. For millennia, rice has been the staple crop for half of the world's population. A major problem of the rice-based diet for humans has been a chronic and damaging vitamin A deficiency. This vitamin is necessary for healthy growth, as well as the health of the eyes and epithelial tissues. Without it, serious health problems, including night blindness, occur.

Two scientists, Ingo Potrykus of the ETH Institute for Plant Science and Peter Beyer of the University of Freiburg in Breisgau, developed a new kind of genetically modified (GM) rice by combining genes of a daffodil and a bacterium and inserting them into the genome of a rice plant. The new grain contains beta-carotene, which produces vitamin A in the body and also turns the grains of rice a golden yellow. The first field of Golden Rice was grown in Louisiana in 2004. Along with the agrotechnology company Syngenta, the two scientists founded the Golden Rice Humanitarian Board to ensure that the technology transfer to developing countries would be free.

In 2006 the journal *Nature Biotechnology* honored the inventors of Golden Rice as two of the most important contributors in their field in the last ten years in the category of agricultural, environmental, and industrial biotechnology. Outstanding leaders honored in all the categories were:

- Society and ethics—Bill and Melinda Gates
- Policy and regulations—Rita Colwell
- Biopharmaceuticals—James Shapiro and Ray Rajotte
- Technology—Ian Wilmut and Keith Campbell
- U.S. biobusiness—Arthur Levinson
- European biobusiness—Dan Vassella
- Biobusiness outside U.S.-European markets—Kiran Mazumdar-Shaw

In the United States, the contributions of Bill and Melinda Gates in the category of society and ethics were especially significant because of their two very large donations totaling more than $800 million for research for HIV/AIDS vaccines and treatment. The donations were made through the Bill and Melinda Gates Foundation.

As you can see from the *Nature Biotechnology* journal's honors categories, biotechnology has become a powerful international industry. As an industry, it is pouring out its sometimes-miraculous and sometimes-controversial and catalytic innovations into our farmlands, barns, and automobiles; into our kitchens, bathrooms, bedrooms, hospitals, and drugstores; and throughout many other areas of our daily lives. Biotechnology today has become big, big business—and it's still growing.

As a participant in the publicly traded financial markets, biotechnology has been a player for only about three decades. In that short time, it has grown to a more-than-$60-billion industry, representing hundreds of products in the pharmaceutical and health care areas alone. Its development is not slowing down, and the future promises to bring even more rapid and amazing growth in biotechnology than any we have yet seen.

What Is Biotechnology?

Is biotechnology simply the application of living organisms to human use? In this sense, humans have used biotechnology for thousands of years. Perhaps its simplest and earliest beginnings were in the use of living cultures of microorganisms of certain bacteria and yeasts to make yogurt, cheese, and bread, and in the applications of specially selected spider webs and molds to help heal infected wounds. To the uninitiated, these early uses no doubt seemed mysterious, magical, powerful, and dangerous, and there is evidence that since prehistoric times shamans in various cultures worldwide have employed biotechnology in various ways in their healing practices.

The field of biotechnology as we know it in the industrial world today continues to be astonishing, powerful, and controversial. Its explosively expanding complexity and growth and its critical importance to the continued life, health, and economy of our planet are almost beyond comprehension, even to sophisticated experts within the field. When we consider what has happened in the field of biotechnology in the last fifty and even the last ten years, and what is likely to develop in this field in the foreseeable future, the words of popular culture serve us well: it's totally awesome and out of sight!

As a result of the great complexity of the biotechnology field today, many people have little, if any, idea of what it involves. Cloning, DNA and stem-cell research, and HIV/AIDS treatments get headlines and sometimes even hour-long TV specials, but they are not fully understood by everyone. Some people equate biotechnology with genetically engineered (GE) or genetically modified foods such as "bionic" tomatoes that last longer before spoiling; others associate biotechnology with now-familiar medical breakthroughs such as test-tube babies and with new techniques for diagnosing cancer and other diseases. Although these examples do fall under the category of biotechnology, the field encompasses much more; it encompasses an enormous, wide range of equally amazing new scientific and technological processes and methods.

We can begin to understand the term *biotechnology* by examining its parts. *Bio* means living organisms or tissues; *technology* is a scientific method of achieving a practical purpose. Thus, *biotechnology*, in simple terms, is scientists using living things to achieve practical purposes.

The U.S. government has defined biotechnology as any technique that uses living organisms or parts of living organisms to:

1. Make or modify products
2. Improve plants or animals
3. Develop microorganisms for specific uses

The government of Canada has defined biotechnology slightly differently. One of its definitions is: "Biotechnology is the utilization of a biological process, be it via microbial plant or animal cells, or their constituents, to provide goods and services."

The European Federation has defined biotechnology as "the integrated use of biochemistry, microbiology, and engineering sciences in order to achieve industrial application of the capabilities of microorganisms, cultured tissue cells, and parts thereof."

Because of its dynamic complexity, the field of biotechnology is, in many ways, still being defined and will continue to be defined by the nature of its growth and development. Nevertheless, all of us need to understand what biotechnology is and what it can mean for human life and the life of our planet. If you are planning a career in this important industry, it is even more crucial that you gain a broad and deep understanding of this field and its relationship to our physical, economic, political, and social lives and the life of our environment. Because biotechnology can have such tremendous power for good and for harm, the greatest challenge for professionals in the field, and for all other human beings, is to use this power wisely: to carefully consider its implications before bringing about irreversible changes to our planet.

The technologies in use today include all of the following.

- Bioprocessing technology
- Biosensors
- Cell culture
- Cloning
- Microarrays
- Monoclonal antibodies

- Nanobiotechnology
- Protein engineering
- Recombinant DNA technology

Among the research and development tools available in these areas are:

- Antisense and RNA interference
- Bioinformatics
- Cell technology
- Cloning
- Gene knockouts
- Genomics
- Microarray technology
- Proteomics
- Stem-cell technology

Historical Perspective

The roots of biotechnology stretch back to the dawn of civilization. At least ten thousand years ago, enterprising ancient people learned that they could improve the quality and quantity of certain foods by controlling the conditions of fermentation, and they employed yeast microorganisms to make wine, beer, and bread.

Early farmers discovered that they could boost the quantity and improve the quality of their agricultural crops by saving and planting the seeds of the most desirable plants. They could observe that the crops that gave the highest yield, that stayed healthiest during periods of drought or disease, and that were the easiest to harvest tended to pass on their characteristics to future generations. Farmers learned that they could speed up this process and perpetuate and strengthen the desirable traits through careful seed selection.

Although farmers were able to use knowledge of genetic characteristics and crossbreeding to advantage, the scientific understanding of these processes was not to develop until centuries later. In the mid-1860s, Gregor Mendel discovered and identified the scientific basis of these early farming techniques while studying the hereditary traits of peas. Mendel's work opened the doors to understanding genetic processes and hybridization. In the twentieth century, with the advantages of sophisticated laboratories and technological equipment, scientists gained a broader understanding of the scientific principles and processes behind natural processes such as fermentation and heredity. For a more complete time line of biotechnology advances, see Appendix A.

Major Branches

We cannot define biotechnology as a single science, nor as a single procedure, technique, or process. Rather, biotechnology is an interdisciplinary field involving a multitude of biotechnological disciplines that draw upon all the life sciences, as well as computer science and engineering. There is no single traditional educational track that will prepare a student for a career in biotechnology.

The work of biotechnology careers can be grouped into some general categories.

- Human health care
- Agriculture and animal health care
- Energy/environmental management

These categories can be broken down into many subcategories, which are expanding on an ongoing basis and which include, but are certainly not limited to, applications of biotechnology in the following areas.

Applications in Human Health Care
- Diagnostics
- Therapeutics
- Regenerative medicine
- Vaccines
- Genomics and proteomics
- Approved biotechnology drugs

Applications in Agriculture and Animal Health Care
- Forest biotechnology
- Animal biotechnology, including applications for human medicine, companion animals, transgenic animals, and environmental and conservation efforts
- Crop biotechnology, including production improvement, impact on developing countries, environmental and economic benefits, and regulations

Applications in Energy and Environmental Management
- Biomass from chemicals, wastes, residues, and fuel crops
- Enhanced oil recovery and nonfossil fuel sources
- Chemicals and solvents
- Decomposition and detoxification of chemicals
- Biosensors and biochips
- Improved microbial systems for environmental control of air, water, and soil

- Extraction of low-grade metals and recovery of valuable metals
- Hydrogen and carbon dioxide production

In addition, there are some important applications in three other areas: food biotechnology, industry and the environment, and biodefense. In food biology, biotechnology has made important contributions in improving raw materials, processing, and testing for food safety.

Important industrial applications include industrial sustainability, biocatalysts, renewable energy, Green plastics, nanotechnology, environmental technology, and industrial enzymes.

In biodefense, biotechnology has made contributions to policy and is considered a strategic asset because of the importance of vaccines, monoclonal antibodies, DNA- or RNA-based therapeutics, detection diagnostics, and other uses.

Current Areas of Research

The numbers of biotechnology companies are growing rapidly, and they are engaged in an enormous variety of endeavors. Listed below are just a few of the multitude of areas of scientific research in which biotechnology companies are involved.

Agricultural products
Anticancer diagnostics and therapeutics
Artificial organ technology
Biocatalysts
Biochemical engineering

Biodefense
Biodiesel fuels
Biosynthesis
Cancer research
Cellular biology
Chemicals
Chromatography
Diagnostics
Enzymology
Epidemiology
Fermentation
Gene synthesis
Genetic engineering
Health care products
High-yield grain products
HIV/AIDS research
Human-made fibers
Hybridoma technology
Immunology
Industrial enzymes
Minerals
Molecular biology
Monoclonal antibodies
Oil- and gas-related research
Organ transplant research and therapy
Pharmaceutical research
Plastics
Products in gram-positive organisms
Protein chemistry

Recombinant DNA products and processes
Resins
Seed inoculants
Stem-cell research

Major investments are being made in biotechnology research all over the world, not only in the United States but also in Canada, Mexico, Latin America, Europe, Asia/Pacific, Africa, Australia— in every country new research laboratories and production companies are appearing rapidly. Competition is keen, and multinational mergers and acquisitions, alliance partnerships, and cooperative ventures of many kinds are uniting research organizations and commercial ventures between Argentina, Brazil, Chile, China, Europe, India, Japan, Russia, Singapore, Thailand, the United States, and many other areas.

Looking Ahead

A career in the field of biotechnology offers almost limitless opportunities for those who choose it for their life's work. If you are a well-educated and well-prepared young scientist, you can have a broad breadth of choices in area of specialization, the kind of research or related work you want to do, the kind of organization you want to work with, and your own short- and long-term goals. In today's world you also have nearly global choice about where you will live and work.

To make the best choices while you are deciding upon your career path, you will want to learn all you can. To make the best ongoing choices as a professional in your field later on, you will want to make sure that you continue to keep up with a thorough knowledge of your field and its industry. This will ensure you understand how its growth and changes are affecting your work and be able to recognize which opportunities are closing and which are opening as you work to build your career and your accomplishments through the years.

2

DEVELOPMENTS IN
MODERN BIOTECHNOLOGY

STEM-CELL RESEARCH, biochips, recombinant DNA, cloning, and dozens of other revolutionary topics regularly punctuate the biotechnology news on television, on radio, in the newspapers, and on the Internet. There is so much happening in the biotechnology field that, if we could see it on the surface of Earth from outer space, it might remind us of Brownian movement. As in Brownian movement, the energy characterizing this field is apparent in an astonishing amount of dynamic activity that is jiggling and bouncing around everywhere. We are seeing a previously unheard-of myriad of scientific endeavors that are acting, reacting, and interacting with each other in as yet unimagined ways, and they are impacting our health care, food, clothing, shelter, farms, businesses, schools, financial markets, and governmental and social institutions at a tremendous rate in nearly every part of the world.

For the twentieth year, the world-recognized professional services company of Ernst & Young has conducted, with the support of the Biotechnology Industry Organization (BIO), Battelle, the State Science and Technology Institute (SSTI), and PMP Public Affairs Consulting, Inc., an extensive report on the state of biotechnology, which it published as *Beyond Borders: The Global Biotechnology Report 2006*. The report emphasizes the unique nature of this industry and the changing conditions worldwide that are bringing it to a new stage of maturity.

The report stated that revenues for the world's publicly traded portions of the industry increased by 30 percent from 2004 to 2005, bringing the total to more than $63 billion. They reported also that, in general, profitability is still an elusive goal, but that the bottom line was much improved by the United States, Canada, and the Asia-Pacific region, which together came about $3 billion closer to that goal.

The recession that began in 2000 and deepened in 2001 had an impact on biotechnology investment and upon hiring as well; but in 2005 a definite upturn was achieved, and it is expected to continue. The U.S. market was stable and stronger in 2005, and stronger product sales were seen, although some companies still planned moves to other countries where labor and tax conditions were more favorable.

In Canada, a 2005 survey by PriceWaterhouseCoopers found that the industry was maturing but that nearly half of Canadian companies surveyed were considering moving part or all of their operations to other countries, unless conditions for business improved, including taxation and other incentives. The European market made a strong showing with approximately 17 percent growth, and the Asia-Pacific market was seen to be increasing in strength through strong competition and an aggressive growth drive, using highly focused strategies to develop innovative, globally competitive companies. In Australia, companies in several areas were making strong product offerings, and in Africa, more countries were trying to foster growth of their own companies, especially in agriculture and biomedical research.

In Canada, the *Canadian Biotechnology Industry Report of 2004* was the first-ever such industry-wide report for that nation. It showed Canada to be a rich source of innovation in the field with 417 core companies, more than 80 percent of which were six or fewer years of age and had fifty or fewer employees, and more than 70 percent of which were focused upon diagnostics and therapeutics product development. This picture of a young industry invested primarily in the medical and pharmaceutical segments of the industry is of interest to government, investors, and job seekers. It shows that in Canada, as in the United States and several of the developed nations, the biotechnology industry is one of great diversity and flexibility. The report provides information on contract research organizations, medical device companies, equipment and diagnostic suppliers, venture capital companies, genomic companies, government departments, and research associations. It is published by *Canadian Biotech News*, which you can contact at www.info @cana dianbiotechnews.com.

An Interdisciplinary Science

Biotechnology is not, technically speaking, a single field, nor is it just an industry. It involves and, in fact, demands many disciplines. It brings together agriculturalists, biologists, botanists, chemists, computer scientists, engineers, pathologists, veterinarians, zoologists, and many, many other specialists.

Specialists from many disciplines are at work in the biotechnology field today. Some of the many areas in which scientists and nonscientists are currently at work in biotechnology-related positions are described in Table 2.1. In some cases, a person's background in two or more of these specializations may form the basis of his or her career.

New ideas, new research projects, new companies, new products, new rules and regulations, new financing, new public reaction and consumption, and millions of communications and transactions are occurring everywhere simultaneously in a dynamic multidisciplinary and multicultural network of global exchange.

Thousands of research and development projects are taking place in Africa, Asia, North and South America, Australia, and Antarctica; and they are being carried out in land laboratories, the oceans, the atmosphere, and in space. They are bringing together scientists, nonscientific specialists, educators and communicators, government officials, and investors from many countries in work that is urgently needed in many areas.

A great deal of the speed of this explosion of activity is due, of course, to the proliferation of and the support provided by high technology computer science and communications—not much of this high-speed exchange or production would be happening at all if it were not for the rapidly developing capacities of the computer and the Internet.

In addition, new pressures such as the enormous increases in our world population, increasing competition for dwindling food and energy-fuel supplies, raging disease epidemics such as HIV/AIDS, and the stresses such as global warming upon our environmental ecology that are becoming more and more apparent are all pushing the scientific world for solutions.

Table 2.1 Disciplines in Which Biotechnologists Work Today

Advertising	Data mining	Microbiology
Agriculture	Developmental biology	Molecular biology
Agronomy	Diagnostics	Nanotechnology
Anatomy	Drug development	Neuroscience
Animal technology	Drug discovery	Nutrition
Anthropology	Ecology	Patent law
Anti-drug abuse	Engineering	Pathology
Archaeology	Environmental science	Pharmacology
Astronomy	Epidemiology	Physics
Atmospheric science	Evolutionary biology	Physiology
Biochemistry	Finance	Postdoctoral research
Biodefense	Genetic engineering	Preclinical development
Biology	Genetic modification	Promotion
Biomedical sciences	Genetics	Proteomics
Biophysics	Genomics	Psychiatry/psychology
Biotechnology	Geoscience	Public health
Biotechnology law	Gerontology/aging	Public information
Botany/plant science	Health care	Public relations
Business management	Immunology	Sales and marketing
Cancer research/	Informatics	Statistical analysis
oncology	Information technology	Structural biology
Cell biology	Journalism	Teaching
Chemistry	Knowledge organization/	Toxicology
Clinical medicine	retrieval	Veterinary medicine
Clinical research	Legal/regulatory affairs	Veterinary research
Computational biology	Manufacturing—QA/QC	Virology
Computational	Marine science	Writing
chemistry	Material science	Zoology
Computer science	Mathematics	
Criminology	Medicine	

Biotechnology is being looked to around the world as one of the most important sources for solutions for many of the world's major desires and needs—in human health, in economics, in agriculture, in the drive for nonfossil fuels and energy sources, and, unfortunately, also in the desire by some people and nations for power over their fellow humans—as in the design of frighteningly powerful biochemical weapons. Awareness of the impact of this field is growing by leaps and bounds; startling news and amazing discoveries are frequent events. There is also a great deal of money and power to be gained or lost in this field, and there is, and will continue to be, a lot of jockeying for position and right-of-way to get to it. Most important of all, in the field of biotechnology there is enormous potential for good or harm for humanity and for the ongoing life of our planet.

How Will You Take Part?

The next question is, what does all of the growth and activity of this field mean for you? Does some of this work draw your interest? What are the most important frontiers? What part might they play in your future, and what part might you play in the future of biotechnology?

If you are considering a career in biotechnology, you will need to gain an overview of the patterns of all the frenetic activity going on in this field today.

The biotechnology field is one that is rich in sources of information and analysis. The Internet alone provides links to websites, e-newsletters, reference sources, and, of course, the direct person-to-person communication of e-mail. In addition, there are hundreds of professional associations, government agencies, commercial organizations, and educational and research institutions that annually publish millions of pages of print materials and thousands of electronic-media information products. There is no lack of information about what is happening in biotechnology and no lack of access to the knowledge that has been achieved in the myriad research projects that have been completed or that are in progress. With all this information, it may, however, be hard to know where to begin or where to focus your plans.

Getting an Overview

Because biotechnology is so dynamic, fast growing, and fast changing, gaining an overview of the field will be very helpful. The descriptions provided in this book will provide some of this for you. In addition, you will find that checking key websites and reviewing e-newsletters and other professional publications will help you become familiar with the character of this global and, in many ways, revolutionary field.

Professional Resources

The appendixes of this book provide a generous, though by no means exhaustive, annotated reference list of associations and professional organizations (Appendixes B and C), a list of colleges and universities that provide solid academic preparation for a career (Appendix D), and a list of electronic and print professional publications by some of the foremost academic, scholarly, and research organizations in the world (Appendix E).

Websites are provided, and you will want to explore the tremendously varied and interesting material that these organizations have published. It is easy to keep up if you subscribe to a weekly newsletter, many of which are offered free by the associations and organizations in the field. Once you have become familiar with a range of the websites, you can select those that serve your specific interests and visit them regularly as you go forward in your career.

Biotechnology Industry Organization

In all the global buzz of this biotechnology beehive, one organization stands out in the United States as a leader, and it is the largest, most comprehensive, and most accessible professional association: the Biotechnology Industry Organization (BIO).

BIO provides an enormous breadth of information about the industry in the United States and globally, and it is an excellent source for professional contacts and for your ongoing continuing education. It holds meetings, seminars, and major national annual conferences and provides in-depth analyses, reports, and papers by industry leaders. It provides news and information on education, careers, fields of research, scientific breakthroughs, changes in laws and regulations, and biotechnology-related activities in all fifty states, as well as in the global community. It also provides career information and job postings; news of new product breakthroughs; testing, production, and marketing of products and services; and major institutional and governmental initiatives.

If you have not already discovered it, you will find this association a satisfying and basic tool for building and maintaining your professional knowledge of the industry. You can access its website by going to www.bio.org.

Developments in Genetic Engineering

Currently, one of the most exciting and publicized branches of biotechnology is genetic engineering (GE), also referred to as genetic modification (GM) or bioengineering, which is involved essentially with changing the DNA of the cells of plants and animals to create forms that will better serve certain selected human needs and, therefore, be more monetarily profitable to produce, as well.

Since the development of sophisticated gene splicing in the mid-1970s, the technique known as *recombinant DNA*, scientists have been able to remove and add genetic material to a cell's DNA. By impregnating the genetic material of plants and animals with "helpful" genes taken from the DNA of other organisms, biotechnologists are creating new kinds of foods.

The U.S. Department of Agriculture frequently issues permits to companies across the country allowing them to field-test genetically engineered crops. Many bioengineered foods have already been developed, and more are in process.

Proponents of plant biotechnology have stated that there has been a decade of widespread use of genetically modified crops and consumption of GM food products raised under the strictest regulations and surveillance from international, national, and local groups of many kinds, and it has been completely safe and successful. In 2006 approximately 8.25 million farmers chose to plant genetically modified crops, and the majority of those were small farmers in developing countries. More than sixty countries were conducting biotechnology plant research for fifty-seven different crops.

Genetically modified (GM) crops were first grown (outside of experimentation) in the United States in 1996. By 2006, three-quarters of all the GM crops being grown worldwide were in Canada and the United States on much larger farms in fewer hands. The third-largest growing area is Mexico and South America. Both China and India have funded major biotechnology initiatives to further their use of GE crops. Genetically modified crops have not been accepted nearly as quickly by growers in Europe, where active consumer and other organizations have urged more caution. GENET, one of the best known of the European NGOs (nongovernmental organizations), has developed a network of information and feedback on genetic engineering. You can get more information about its work at www.genet-info.org.

High-yield agriculture in the last half of the twentieth century involved the increasing use of vast amounts of chemical fertilizers and pesticides. These toxic chemicals have been extremely costly to farmers and, in addition, often have had devastating effects on the environment. Hoping to reduce the need for chemical fertilizers and pesticides, scientists have created plants that can repel pests and help to fertilize themselves.

Agronomists also are using genetic engineering to strengthen plants against diseases and harmful environmental conditions that attack them, such as alkaline deposits, drought, earth metals, soil salinity, and soil that lacks air.

Some of the genetically engineered foods that have been produced are a type of rice that has greater protein content, wheat that can help fertilize itself by producing its own nitrogen, and tomatoes that have more pulp and less water. Biotechnologists have also experimented with using gene splicing to make chickens bigger, pigs leaner, and crops such as strawberries and tomatoes resistant to frost damage.

Controversies and Ethical Issues

Although the positive potential and exciting possibilities of biotechnology seem virtually limitless, there are legitimate concerns about the expanding scope and power of this science cluster and especially about the new branch of bioengineering.

The science of bioengineering has tremendous potential for good; it can, however, just as easily be used irresponsibly. There is deep concern about the eventual effects of genetically modifying living things because it is impossible to know what unexpected results may occur as time goes by. Therefore, the testing component of the field of genetic engineering is as important as its innovations, and jobs in this area carry enormous responsibility.

Environmentalists are concerned about what will happen when genetically engineered plants and animals enter the earth's delicate ecosystem and food chain. Many people predict that creating genetically altered organisms will further reduce the Earth's biological diversity, resulting in "superweeds" that will threaten current plant species and produce unforeseen allergens and toxins in the foods we eat. Other people question the morality of manipulating the genetic makeup of animals. Since the Human Genome Project completed the human gene map in 2003, many people have also been afraid that scientists would use biotechnological methods to manipulate human genetics to control who and what will be born.

Obviously there is much work to be done to find ways to control the use of genetically modified crops, which, while more financially profitable than the traditional crops in many cases, have not yet withstood the test of time. In addition, some growers who do not want to use the GM seed are complaining that they are not able to maintain their traditional crops in some places because the genetically modified grains in nearby fields are contaminating their crops through pollination and by seeds carried by wind, birds, and other animals. Some bitter lawsuits have been begun to try to impose limits on the use of the GM crops.

In May of 2006, Representative Dennis Kucinich (Ohio-10th) introduced the Genetically Engineered Food Right to Know Act

(H.R.5269) to require labeling of genetically engineered foods, which are labeled in many other countries, including the European Union, Japan, China, Australia, New Zealand, and South Korea.

At the international level, the World Health Organization and the Food and Agriculture Organization of the United Nations are active in addressing and regulating food safety as well as health and disease issues, usually in cooperation with the national organizations of the broad spectrum of member states.

In the United States, ethical controversy surrounds the area of stem-cell research because some research has been carried out using stem cells from human embryos, and some groups want to do more of this. Other groups consider a human embryo to be a human being and to have all the ethical, legal, and religious status, rights, and protections of a viable human individual.

The Union of Concerned Scientists is one of a number of respected organizations that bring ethical and safety concerns to public knowledge and that publicize information bearing upon new experiments. There are many others, sometimes referred to as "watchdog organizations," in the United States and in other countries. It is worthwhile to keep up on these organizations' concerns and check their publications frequently.

From a scientific standpoint, bioengineering is an extremely exciting field. Along with its power for change, it raises difficult questions. Scientists and students interested in this branch of biotechnology will need to consider social, economic, ethical, environmental, religious, and other value-related implications of genetic manipulation before taking actions to utilize its power. They will also need to be prepared to explain and defend their innovations and to provide extensive evidence of their safety and usefulness to the hopeful but wary public officials, scientific community peers, and general public that await their benefits.

Biotechnology and Human Health

No segment of the broad biotechnology field is as important to the human condition as the segment that deals with human health. The hopes of millions of people are focused on the research that could bring us vaccines or cures for HIV/AIDS, avian flu, cancer, malaria, tuberculosis, diabetes, and a host of other diseases and health problems. Research in these areas has been catapulted into a new kind of future—seemingly almost within our reach—by the new methods and discoveries of biotechnology.

Monoclonal Antibody Technology

One very important area of the new biotechnology research is that of monoclonal antibodies. Substances that are foreign to the body, such as viruses, disease-causing bacteria, and other infectious agents, have structural features jutting from their surfaces. These features, called *antigens*, are recognized by the body's immune system as invaders. Our bodies' natural defenses against these infectious agents are antibodies, proteins that seek out the antigens and help to destroy them.

Antibodies have two very useful characteristics. First, they are extremely specific; that is to say, each antibody binds to and attacks one particular antigen. Second, some antibodies, once they are activated by the occurrence of a disease, continue to offer resistance against that disease. For example, once you have had the chicken pox, you should have antibodies that will not let it occur again in your body.

That second characteristic of antibodies makes it possible to create vaccines. A vaccine is a preparation of killed or weakened bacteria or viruses that, when introduced into a person's body, stimulates the production of antibodies against the antigens it contains.

It is the first trait, the specific nature of antibodies, that makes monoclonal antibody technology so valuable to us. Not only can antibodies be used therapeutically to protect against disease, they can also help to diagnose a wide variety of illnesses. Furthermore, they can be used to detect the presence of drugs, viral and bacterial products, and other unusual or abnormal substances in the blood.

Because there is such a diversity of uses for all these disease-fighting substances, their production in pure quantities has long been the focus of scientific investigation. During most of the twentieth century, the conventional method had been to inject a laboratory animal with an antigen and then, when antibodies had been formed, collect those antibodies from the blood serum. There are two problems with this method. First, it yields *antiserum*, an antibody containing blood serum, which is comprised of undesired substances. Second, it provides a very small amount of usable antibody. However, by using modern monoclonal antibody technology, scientists today are able to produce much, much larger amounts of pure antibodies.

Bioprocess Technology

Modern bioprocess technology, like many other applications of biotechnology, is an extension of ancient techniques for developing useful products by taking advantage of natural biological activities. When our early ancestors made alcoholic beverages, they used a bioprocess—the combination of yeast cells and cereal grains. This combination formed a fermentation system in which the organisms consumed the grain for their own growth and, while doing so, produced by-products (alcohol and carbon dioxide gas) that helped to make the beverage.

Although certainly more advanced, today's bioprocess technology is based upon the same principle: combining living matter (whole organisms or enzymes) with nutrients under the conditions necessary to make the desired end product.

Several areas of commercial biotechnology have utilized specific bioprocesses. These include the production of enzymes used for such things as antibodies, food processing, and waste management.

As techniques and instrumentation become more and more refined, bioprocesses may have applications in many other areas where chemical processes are now used. Bioprocesses offer several advantages over chemical processes: bioprocesses require lower temperature, pressure, and pH (a measure of acidity); they can use renewable resources as raw materials; and far greater quantities can be produced with much less energy consumption.

Nanotechnology Products

Another fascinating new area of research is in the use of nanotechnology. In just a few years its use has become widespread, particularly in the pharmaceutical industry.

The Center for Responsible Nanotechnology (CRN) has said that a basic definition of nanotechnology is "engineering of functional systems at the molecular scale." It is also called *molecular manufacturing*, and it is becoming recognized as the possible basis of another fundamental industrial revolution.

Richard Feynman, Nobel prize winner in physics, envisioned "the possibility of maneuvering things atom by atom" to make tiny functioning factories and vehicles that could perform complex tasks. He stated that "[This] is not an attempt to violate any laws; it is something, in principle, that can be done; but in practice, it has not been done because we are too big."

To try to grasp the scale of nanotechnology, one nanometer is one-billionth of a meter, and a single page of the book you are holding in your hand is approximately one hundred thousand nanometers thick.

The term *nanotechnology* was popularized in the 1980s, especially because of the writing of K. Eric Drexler, pioneer in the study of productive nanosystems and their products. His book *Engines of Creation: The Coming Era of Nanotechnology* brought the concept to the general public. Drexler continued to build upon the concept and created a foundation of ideas, proposing the use of mechanochemistry guided by molecular machine systems in creating revolutionary devices such as complete motors and computers that were tinier than a cell. In 1991 he received his Ph.D. in molecular nanotechnology from the Massachusetts Institute of Technology (MIT), the first degree of its kind. Often called the godfather of nanotechnology, Drexler was the founder and longtime chairman of the Foresight Institute. At first Drexler's ideas were not accepted, but, as time went by, the scientific community was able to develop simple structures on a molecular scale, and Drexler's concepts were no longer considered to be science fiction.

The U.S. National Nanotechnology Initiative was established in 2003, and although it is limited in its scope, it would fund nanotechnology development for projects smaller than one hundred nanometers.

Recognition of the potential of nanotechnology has begun to spread throughout the political and popular worlds. Its potential is considered to be as great as the invention of electricity or the computer, and it can be applied in broad areas of human life, including production to meet basic needs of food, clothing, and shelter; communication; transportation; and the military.

In this last area, it presents a potential for far more powerful weaponry and, therefore, will require solidly responsible international efforts for surveillance and control.

The CRN has said that this technology could come about much sooner than the twenty or thirty years that are usually estimated. Because of the rapid progress that has already been enabled by the new technologies in optics, nanolithography, mechanochemistry, and 3D prototyping, the CRN has urged preparation now in research, planning, and governing bodies to meet four important questions: 1) Who will own the technology? 2) Will it be heavily restricted or widely available? 3) What will it do to the gap between rich and poor? 4) How can dangerous weapons be controlled and perilous arms races be prevented?

In 2006 the U.S. Food and Drug Administration (FDA) set up a task force to advise on drugs produced using nanotechnology. The task force will recommend ways to "fill any policy or knowledge gaps" and will focus especially on any health threats that could result from medications using the new technology. Many biotech companies have jumped in to use nanotechnology applications to develop new or reformulate old therapies, because by changing a drug's dose to microscopic-sized particles, researchers are able to alter the way the drug works in the human body. This gives drug manufacturers new opportunities and opens possibilities for new kinds of testing and follow-up before new forms are released for use by the general public.

Nanotechnology news publications have developed rapidly on the Internet and in print and include: *Nanobiotech News, Nanotechnology Now, Nanotechnology Law and Business,* and *Nano Today.*

Focused and ongoing information about the nanotechnology sector of the biotechnology industry is available by going to www.crnano.org for the excellent website of the CRN, and a career website specializing in nanotechnology jobs can be accessed at www.tinytechjobs.com.

HIV/AIDS: Fourteen Thousand New Infections Every Day

The wildfire spread of the pandemic of AIDS (Acquired Immune Deficiency Syndrome) is the most devastating international health threat currently facing the world.

Since AIDS was first recognized as a disease in 1983, millions of people around the world have been infected with the human immunodeficiency virus (HIV) that causes AIDS. According to the Global Health Organization, in 2006 more than 38,600,000 people of a total world population of 6,446,131,400 were living with HIV/AIDS. In the United States alone, the Kaiser Family Foundation reported that by 2004, nearly a million men, women, and children had been infected with HIV/AIDS and more than half of them had died.

Increasingly, in the last few years, biotechnology has played a crucial role in slowing the spread of AIDS as well as in treating it and slowing the death rates in the parts of the world where the new medications are available and can be afforded. In the developed countries, in particular, medication is available that has greatly extended the life spans of those with HIV/AIDS. In poorer areas, however, the death rate is extremely high, and a diagnosis of HIV/AIDS is almost inevitably a death sentence.

Medically, some significant gains have been made. Using monoclonal antibody technology, biomedical researchers developed laboratory tests to show whether blood has been contaminated with the HIV virus. This has helped slow the spread of AIDS by informing people if they are HIV carriers and enabling more effective screening of donated blood.

New drugs such as the antiretroviral therapies have been developed as treatments for HIV and the infectious diseases that accompany it. Major pharmaceutical companies are using biotechnology techniques in an effort to develop an AIDS vaccine. In 2000 there were only two vaccine projects being tested; by 2006 there were four. Efforts to develop a vaccine have not yet been successful, partly because the virus is changing, but advances in knowledge and techniques have been achieved. Because HIV occurs in different forms, it is unlikely that a single vaccine will be effective against all of them, and new kinds of vaccines are being researched.

Both private and public funding is being used to support research, testing, and treatment worldwide. In 2006, renewed strength and incentive were provided by the Bill and Melinda Gates Foundation in the donation of $287 million to create an international network of scientists pursuing solutions. Also in 2006, the International AIDS Vaccine Initiative (IAVI) and the Global HIV Vaccine Enterprise launched an international forum to foster international cooperation and communication on AIDS research and advances. IAVI was awarded $23.7 million of the Gates Foundation funding to pursue novel virus vectors through the T-Cell Vaccine and Research Development Consortium.

Major challenges in the constant struggle to control the AIDS pandemic include the fact that there are very few facilities in some of the developing countries to pursue research and testing, although these have been increasing; and private enterprise has been discouraged from investing greater amounts of money because the populations with the greatest needs for vaccines and for treatment of existing cases are in areas that have the least resources and supporting funds.

The proportions of the struggle to defeat the AIDS pandemic make this a profoundly challenging and worthwhile frontier in biotechnology. If you are interested in learning more about the state of HIV/AIDS research and the possibilities of work in this field, some key information sources are listed below, which will, in turn, lead you to many, many more.

- Cornell University, Department of Microbiology and Immunology, www.cornell.edu.com
- HIV/AIDS Global Health Database, www.globalhealth facts.org
- HIV Vaccines and Microbicides Resource Tracking Working Group, www.hivresourcetracking.org
- IAVI, Database of Ongoing Trials of Vaccines, Career Information, www.iavi.org
- Kaiser Family Foundation, www.statehealthfacts.org

Other Medical Frontiers

Many other serious diseases are the subjects of major investment of work and funds in the biotechnology field. Ongoing research in tuberculosis, which now claims 14,602,353 cases worldwide, and malaria, with 408,388,001 cases, are of extreme importance. In addition, solutions to the many deadly and debilitating forms of cancer; diabetes; heart, lung, and kidney disease; and hundreds of other diseases are being researched.

The creation of new medicinal drugs follows a pattern of development: first, scientists must determine what specific drugs are required. Then they plan their design, carry out experiments, test and retest the findings, and go through a lengthy process of registration and permits for development and testing of products once they are created. Until only recently, it was expected that twenty years was a reasonable length of time for development of a major new vaccine, but this estimate has been speeded up considerably. High costs of human suffering, of medical treatment, of research and development, pressure everyone involved for speed. Many industry experts predict another "explosion" of discoveries leading to many new pharmaceutical products that will far exceed the substantial growth in drug development over the last fifty years.

Professionals in the health field, as well as their patients, already owe much to biotechnology. Vitamin B12, steroids, and many birth control pills originate from biotechnological sources. Human insulin was the first recombinant DNA-derived product to become commercially available. It was first marketed in 1982.

The Biotechnology Industry Organization reports other important studies that biotechnologists are making to keep us healthy, some of which are described in the sections that follow.

Fighting Heart Disease

Each year, approximately 1.1 million people suffer heart attacks. More than 400,000 of those attacks are fatal. Many of these patients can be saved from death or permanent disability with a genetically engineered drug called *tissue plasminogen activator*, or TPA.

TPA is a natural human protein that dissolves blood clots. It occurs naturally in the blood but in amounts too small to stop a heart attack. When a heart attack strikes, doctors may inject genetically engineered TPA into the patient's blood. This protein travels to the clot, breaking it up within minutes and restoring blood flow to the heart muscle. By quickly restoring blood flow, TPA helps prevent life-threatening damage to the heart muscle.

New Weapons for the War on Cancer

Major investments have been made in the nation's war on cancer since the early 1970s, but cancer is still second only to heart disease as a killer. Each year, more than one million Americans develop some form of cancer, and more than five hundred thousand people die from the different forms of the disease.

Biotechnology is used to treat cancer in three ways. Some genetically engineered proteins, called *lymphokines*, appear to attack cancer cells directly, or they may trigger the body's immune system to attack the cancer. Other genetically engineered proteins, called *growth factors*, appear to push cancer cells to maturity, slowing the rampant reproduction. Finally, monoclonal antibodies armed with radioactive material, cancer drugs, or other poisons search out and destroy cancer cells.

A genetically engineered lymphokine, named alpha-interferon, is used to treat people with hairy cell leukemia, a cancer that several hundred Americans develop each year. Before the use of alpha-interferon, a diagnosis of hairy cell leukemia was a death sentence. People with the disease required frequent blood transfusions and became highly susceptible to infections. There were no effective long-term treatments. Now, alpha-interferon can restore people with hairy cell leukemia to normal health. The protein appears to bind to the surface of the cancer cell, halting its growth.

Immune-based therapies are being used for cancer treatments as well as for treating AIDS. Doctors are looking to other genetically engineered lymphokines to treat these patients. Interleukin-2 activates special white blood cells, called *killer cells*, which can destroy cancer cells. These activated killer cells are providing treatment for people with advanced melanoma and kidney cancers.

Another group of proteins, called *colony stimulating factors*, trigger the production and activity of cells of the immune system. Colony stimulating factors are proving useful in marshalling the body's defenses against cancer and AIDS. They may also help restore normal blood production in patients with severe anemia or those undergoing bone marrow transplantation.

In 2005 the *New England Journal of Medicine* reported on success with the new drug Herceptin, which is effective for breast cancers linked to the HER2 gene. Herceptin cut the risk of recurring cancer by 50 percent in trials at the Mayo Clinic, the European Herceptin Adjuvant (HERA trial), and others.

Multiple new cancer drugs are being developed and tested by the private and public sectors. The National Cancer Institute (NCI) maintains the NCI Registry of ongoing trials where you can learn about the more than a thousand trials in progress, as you consider what kind of work you would like to do and whether any of these areas of research are of interest to you. To access the NCI Registry, go to www.thewellnesscommunity.org/clinical.trials/vwc.asp.

Other Diseases

In addition to heart disease, cancer, AIDS, and diabetes, there are hundreds of other diseases that biotechnology will help to treat in the coming years. Here is a small sample of some of the other conditions for which biotechnology products are available or under development.

• **Pituitary dwarfism.** Of the approximately two hundred types of dwarfism, pituitary dwarfism can be successfully treated with regular injections of human growth hormone. Genetically engineered growth hormone provides greater quantities than were available previously, and it also provides a safer, virus-free therapy for treating this particular type of dwarfism.

• **Hemophilia.** The human body has twelve identified blood clotting factors, designated as Factors I–XII. Hemophiliacs' bodies cannot produce enough of a protein called Factor VIII, which controls blood clotting, and they can suffer from life-threatening profuse internal bleeding and hemorrhages from even minor wounds. Transfusions of Factor VIII from human blood can control the disorder, but these transfusions contain only 1 percent Factor VIII and can also transmit viral diseases. Some hemophiliacs were infected with HIV from therapeutic blood transfusions in the early 1980s, and they can still get hepatitis from contaminated Factor VIII.

Today, monoclonal antibody technology is used to make Factor VIII that is 99 percent pure, and studies are under way with genetically engineered Factor VIII, which is completely pure and incapable of transmitting disease.

In addition, research is under way as of 2006 in gene therapy that may provide a solution. For information on ongoing research and related careers, go to the website of the National Hemophilia Association at www.hemophilia.org.

• **Anemia.** Hundreds of thousands of people suffer each year from anemia associated with a variety of conditions, such as chronic renal failure, AIDS, and side effects of cancer chemotherapy. People who are on kidney dialysis or who are undergoing cancer therapy generally suffer from anemia and must receive blood transfusions, which always carry some risk of infectious disease. Several biotechnology companies have developed genetically engineered erythropoietin, also called *hemopoietin*, or EPO, a natural human hormone that stimulates the production of red blood cells and is useful in treating anemia.

• **Organ transplant rejection.** When a patient receives a kidney or other transplanted organ, the patient's immune system may recognize it as an invader and attack it. Such rejection can cause a transplant to fail, which can be fatal. Using monoclonal antibodies, doctors can eliminate T cells, elements of the immune system responsible for organ rejection. The patient will also receive medications for the rest of her or his life to help the body resist infection and continue to accept the transplanted organ.

• **Common cold.** Medicine has conquered many common bacterial diseases with antibiotics, but antibiotics are useless against viral diseases, one of which is the common cold. Ongoing research is devoted to finding a cure for this expensive ailment, which causes millions of lost school and work days each year. In 2006 two major pharmaceutical companies, ViroPharma and Schering-Plough, were at work on antiviral drugs targeting the picornaviruses, which are causes of most common colds. One marketed drug, Pleconaril, had proven effective in oral form but was found to have some dangerous side effects, so research is still being done.

Interferon is a natural protein produced by the body's immune system. As a cold remedy it is being administered intranasally and, as of 2006, was in use in Eastern Europe, Russia, and Japan, but not yet in other parts of the world.

Advances in Diagnosis

In addition to providing new drugs, biotechnology has added to the physician's trove of diagnostic tools.

Monoclonal Antibodies in Diagnosis

A number of biotechnology companies are using monoclonal antibodies in diagnostic tests. Because monoclonal antibodies bind specifically to certain targets, they are generally more effective than conventional diagnostic tools in identifying the cause and location of disease. To cite just a few examples, monoclonal antibodies are used in diagnostic procedures for hepatitis, venereal disease, and bacterial infections. They are also used in some home pregnancy-test kits.

Use of monoclonal antibodies enables doctors to evaluate certain conditions of the human body with a clarity unimaginable even twenty years ago. A physician can inject a patient with monoclonal antibodies that carry minute amounts of radioactive material. The antibodies then attach to their target, such as a tumor or heart muscle that has been damaged by a heart attack. The doctor uses a computerized scanning device to locate and study the diseased tissue so that an appropriate course of therapy can be planned.

Recombinant DNA technology allows physicians to identify specific genes, enabling the doctors to diagnose genetic disorders such as cystic fibrosis. Recombinant techniques also are used to detect HIV infection and may someday be used to diagnose a variety of other infectious diseases.

Scope of Biomedical Advances

The speed of research growth in biotechnological applications for the prevention, treatment, and curing of disease is so phenomenal that it is literally giving new hope to millions of patients and their families worldwide. It is also spearheading phenomenal new financial investment in biotechnical pharmaceutical and other health-related firms. Listed below are some of the major human health areas in which biotechnology research has already produced great gains and in which important research is ongoing.

AIDS/HIV
Allergies and asthma
Alzheimer's disease
Anemia
Autoimmune diseases
Avian flu (bird flu; avian influenza)
Cancer of many types
Cardiovascular disease
Chronic granulomatous disease
Congenital heart disease
Crohn's disease
Cushing's disease
Diabetes
Fungal infections
Genital warts
Heart attacks
Hemophilia
Hepatitis
Herpes viruses
Human growth hormone deficiency
Infertility
Influenza
Leukemia
Lyme disease
Lymphomatous meningitis

Malaria
Multiple sclerosis
Non-Hodgkin's lymphoma
Organ-transplant rejection
Osteoarthritis
Pituitary dwarfism
Rheumatoid arthritis
Schistosomiasis
Severe combined immunodeficiency disease (SCID)
Tuberculosis

Disease Prevention

Although many of the therapeutic and diagnostic uses of biotechnology may seem absolutely marvelous today, they may someday appear to be relatively crude. The real promise of the new biology is in helping scientists understand the cause of disease so that health care professionals will better be able to prevent most diseases.

Powerful new vaccines are being developed by biotechnology companies and pharmaceutical firms against a host of infectious diseases, in addition to HIV/AIDS. For example, a genetically engineered vaccine against hepatitis B, a viral disease contracted by more than two hundred thousand people each year, has been made available to doctors in recent years.

Developing nations can receive the greatest impacts from genetically engineered vaccines, where millions of their people die or suffer chronic illness from viral and parasitic diseases such as malaria and schistosomiasis. Scientists are learning to use genetic engineering to mix the genes of many infectious agents to produce single vaccines that can be used to immunize people against more than one disease at a time.

Developed countries, too, have much to gain in disease prevention. Heart disease, for example, can be greatly reduced by lowering the amount of cholesterol-laden food people consume. The risk of certain kinds of cancer can be reduced with a low-fat, high-fiber diet. Biotechnology companies are using genetic engineering to develop foods and food ingredients that are still appealing but are more healthful for the consumer.

Treating Genetic Disorders

Biotechnology also presents the possibility of correcting genetic disorders. One such disorder is severe combined immunodeficiency disease (SCID). Caused by an insufficient amount of a single protein, SCID is a hereditary disorder that was brought to public attention by media coverage of David, the boy in the "plastic bubble." David's life had to be so safeguarded from infection that he lived in a sterile, sealed plastic room. Television shows and movies were made about him and his fascinating, but very difficult, lifestyle. People all over the world saw what it was like to have to live so removed from other people. Now biotechnology has provided a means of treating this condition, which can be cured by replacing the gene that codes for the deficient protein.

Human Gene Therapy and Bioethics

Although replacing missing or defective genes in a person with a genetic disorder may restore normal function to the individual, the person might still pass on the genetic defect to his or her children. Biotechnology research is progressing toward eliminating certain genetic defects in reproductive cells to prevent offspring from inheriting various kinds of disorders. However, this research raises ethical and legal questions about who can be allowed to decide which genes should be passed to future generations and how these treatments should be regulated.

Dr. John Fletcher is professor of biomedical ethics and religious studies, founder of the Center for Bioethics at the University of Virginia School of Medicine, pioneer in the field of bioethics, and former director of Bioethics at the National Institutes of Health. He has stated that he believes human gene therapy can be used without violating ethical principles. "If you had the power not only to prevent a genetic disorder, but to protect the next generation, would you want to take that step? Most people would say 'yes,'" Fletcher said. But Fletcher also said that doctors and patients must "keep the line drawn between treating real diseases that cause death and pain and suffering, and [getting into the area of] trying to engineer perfect people."

We are living at a time when some of the answers to elusive questions about fundamental biological processes may soon be found with the help of biotechnology. Using more powerful methods than ever before, many of which were not even dreamed of a short time ago, biotechnologists are changing our world in some fundamental ways that may also be changing the world for all the generations to come.

3

BASICS OF A BIOTECHNOLOGY CAREER

WHEN YOU THINK of a career in biotechnology, you may think of it with a certain attached glamour or mystique. Certainly this field can have connotations of importance and international sophistication, along with the mystery and magic of being on the cutting edge of human knowledge.

It is true that many of this field's achievements were unheard of only a short time ago. Today's scientific realities will no doubt rapidly give way to the discoveries of the coming decades, many of which are expected to be as astonishing as if a science fiction film had suddenly come true.

While these facts contribute to a glamorous aura, the jobs in this adventurous-sounding field also have their decidedly mundane side. For biotechnology firms to operate efficiently, there are somewhat standardized job titles that entail well-defined, down-to-earth duties and specific entry prerequisites. Although there is flexibility and the job titles will vary a little bit, these job categories, titles, and descriptions of responsibilities are recognizable in the majority of research organizations.

It is worthwhile to review them and see how the jobs in the traditional hierarchy of responsibility work together in a supportive structure in most research labs.

What Research Biologists Do

Research biologists form the mainstay of the industry and specialize in many kinds of research. Nearly a third of the research workers in biotechnology are molecular biologists and immunologists. Most molecular biologists focus on animal and bacterial systems because this research is most applicable to human health. Substantial funding for molecular biology comes from the National Institutes of Health. Immunologists are also greatly involved in the development of hybridomas (the cells produced by fusing two cells of different origins) to create monoclonal antibodies. More recently, the employment of plant molecular biologists has been increasing, with the redirection of agricultural research toward molecular biological techniques.

Bioprocess engineers, biochemists, and microbiologists develop methods of producing biotechnology products in large quantities. The demand for these specialties will increase as products are readied for production.

Microbiologists study bacteria, yeast, and other microorganisms. They identify microbes with particular characteristics for industrial processes. Microbiologists also identify optimum growth conditions for microorganisms and the conditions for their production.

Cell culture specialists perform similar functions for plant and animal cells grown in tissue culture. Tissue culture is becoming increasingly important for the processing of useful products. Expertise in working with tissue culture is much in demand.

Bioprocess engineers design systems to approximate conditions identified by the microbiologists. Bioprocess engineering is related to chemical engineering. One of the main tasks undertaken by bioprocess engineers is the design of fermentation vats and the various vessels used for bioprocessing (bioreactors) that hold the microorganisms that will produce given products. Bioprocess engineers are required for the next stage of production, too, involving the recovery, purification, and quality control of products. Many of these products are extremely fragile, making purification a difficult and highly demanding job.

Job Titles and Descriptions

The following basic outline provides a general idea of the common traditional job titles and positions in biotechnology research. Companies engaged in biotechnology-related research and development may differ in the employment opportunities they offer, the education and experience histories they require, and the responsibilities of members of their personnel teams at particular job levels. The following job descriptions highlight one position each from a group of research families—a research family being a collection of jobs that call for the performance of similar types of activities.

Lab Assistant I, II, and III

A lab assistant I is responsible for performing a wide variety of research/laboratory tasks and experiments under general supervision. This could involve making detailed observations, analyzing data, and interpreting results in written reports and summaries.

Duties also could include maintaining laboratory equipment and keeping an inventory of supplies.

This job classification usually is filled by graduates from two- or four-year programs that provide basic backgrounds in biology. Some firms will hire individuals with only high school diplomas or equivalent experience who have a minimum of zero to one year of relevant laboratory background.

Lab assistants are not "gofers." In some situations they could have their own projects, although this is not as common a practice in commercial/industrial laboratories as it is in those at universities.

A lab assistant carries out routine, day-to-day laboratory procedures. Many employers realize that lab assistants will be more productive if they do not have to repeat the same activity all the time. Therefore, this first-level lab assistant can be responsible for a variety of procedures such as preparing the solutions, chemicals, and tools that everyone senior to this job level utilizes. The lab assistant should be considered an important part of the whole laboratory picture.

Lab assistants must accomplish increasing skills as they move up in rank from I to III. Prior experience counts if someone wants to advance from lab assistant I to lab assistant II. Lab assistant III is the level at which a laboratory manager or a person who has only a bachelor's degree peaks and stops. It is not unusual to find someone settling in at this position for five years or more.

Research Associate I, II, III, IV, and V

A research associate I is responsible, in collaboration with others, usually in a project team, for research and development for products and projects.

He or she makes detailed observations, analyzes data, and interprets results. A worker at this level may exercise technical creativity and discretion in the design, execution, and interpretation of experiments that contribute to projects. This research associate prepares technical reports and summaries, and the job also calls for keeping up-to-date and staying familiar with the industry's current scientific literature.

People management, specifically of lab assistants, is another responsibility of research associates. For example, only lab assistants, not research associates, prepare solutions, chemicals, and DNA and RNA tools for everyone's use.

It is important to remember that beginning job classifications are usually very flexible. Some people who would be associates II in one company may be labeled assistant III at another. It also is not that unusual to find research associates who are doing more demanding work than those employees who are classified as scientists.

Years of experience, the nature of one's independent research, and the excellence ratings of one's experiments are factors propelling a person up the ladder from associate I to associate IV. While a B.S. in a scientific discipline is often sufficient to get a good position when starting out, research associates who anticipate successful career growth will plan to earn a Ph.D. degree.

Postdoctoral Research Scientist I and II

A postdoctoral research scientist is responsible for the design, development, execution, and implementation of scientific research, usually involving a large research team.

He or she investigates the feasibility of applying a wide variety of scientific principles and theories to patented inventions and products. This biotechnologist maintains extensive knowledge of state-of-the-art principles and theories. A postdoctoral research scientist also contributes to the scientific literature of the field and to professional conferences, writing research papers for publication—sometimes called "white papers"—and presenting workshops, seminars, speeches, and other presentations for peers at major meetings, conferences, and workshops.

The educational prerequisite for this position is a Ph.D. in a scientific discipline. Employers prefer postdoctoral research scientists who have had experience in a research environment. Hiring officials expect job candidates to demonstrate potential for technical proficiency, creativity, cooperative abilities with others, excellent communication skills, and the talent and ability for independent thought.

Generally, a postdoctoral research scientist I is a person who has just received his or her Ph.D. A postdoctoral research scientist II is an individual with two to three years of professional experience.

Scientist I, II, III, and IV

A scientist has the same duties as a postdoctoral research scientist. In addition, he or she may coordinate interdepartmental activities and research efforts. The scientist uses professional concepts, knowledge, and skills to solve a broad range of difficult problems in creative and practical ways within the scope of company or departmental policies, procedures, and goals.

The requirements for scientist I are a B.S. or M.S. in a scientific discipline and preferably one to three or more years of experience in a research environment. A Ph.D. is helpful for advancement and may be required for a scientist I position by most companies. Different companies have different criteria, but for the most part, several years of on-the-job accomplishments separate the scientist II, scientist III, and scientist IV levels. Some firms use the categories of assistant scientist and full scientist to classify these levels. To move up at all in these levels, a person basically must show employers what he or she has accomplished and what he or she plans on achieving further.

Merit often helps a bright scientist advance at a faster pace than normal. If, for example, you were twenty-four years old, you had just received your Ph.D., and, in one year, you had found a clone that was worth a great deal of money for your company, you could disregard the years-on-the-job requirement usually needed for upgrading your scientist classification. You probably would become a scientist IV right away, once management officials had realized that you were an independent starter and could perhaps also inspire other scientists in the organization.

Associate Scientific Director

By the time a person works up to the job of associate scientific director, he or she may actually be at the point of leaving the immediate, hands-on work of the laboratory. In fact, the higher a person goes up this ladder of position titles, the more the supervisory and paperwork tasks will increase, and responsibility for actually doing practical work in the laboratory will diminish.

The ultimate transition away from the laboratory bench is at the level of a higher scientist or associate scientific director position. The chance of anyone at either of these levels doing any practical research work is minimal.

Associate scientific directors organize and manage groups of people. They establish what their personnel will work on, determine which directives are or are not panning out, and decide whom to hire or fire or promote. Some companies assign associate scientific directors to management of specific projects.

Scientific Director

The scientific director is responsible for managing the activities of an entire scientific/engineering group in the research, design, and development of an organization's products, projects, and programs. This biotechnologist conducts and works with others on basic research that is relevant to long-term objectives and concerns. He or she writes and reviews manuscripts for publication. Other duties involve developing strategies to ensure effective achievement of scientific goals and monitoring and evaluating the completion of tasks and projects. The scientific director will be responsible for putting together budgets for capital expenditures and labor. This official also participates with other top managers to establish company policies. He or she makes the final decisions on administrative or operational matters. It is not unusual for companies to assign different scientific directors the overall responsibility for the organization's efforts in different fields of interest.

A person who is entertaining thoughts of being a scientific director will need to meet the following qualifications. He or she needs a Ph.D. in a related scientific discipline. His or her résumé should feature a minimum of ten years of related work experience and some management background. The job candidate must have been recognized for individual scientific accomplishments. He or she also must be willing to work very hard—sixty-hour workweeks are not out of the ordinary for scientific directors in the biotechnology industry.

Project Manager and Technical Services Manager

Although some experts consider project managers and technical services managers in the overall research category, other authorities question their presence in this grouping.

A project manager is responsible for providing oversight to maximize the effective use of resources. He or she facilitates information flow between research team members, project leaders, senior management, and corporate clients. The goal of the project manager is to maintain positive interaction with the client and initiate and coordinate the decision-making process. The direction given by a project manager is administrative rather than technical. His or her supervision is indirect rather than direct.

The educational prerequisite for this position is a B.S. or M.S. in a scientific discipline or equivalent. The expected work history needed to fill this job is a minimum of three to five years of industrial experience in multiple disciplines. The job applicant must have previous know-how in overseeing projects.

A technical services manager is at the master's level. He or she is knowledgeable in communicating about the services needed with management and all levels of workers in the project or department.

Scientific Jobs Outside of Product Research and Development

There are a number of jobs available in the biotechnology field that although still scientific in nature do not fall strictly within the domain of product research and development. Several of these jobs are described below.

Quality Control Workers

Many of those involved in quality control usually can be found working at companies that manufacture pharmaceuticals using recombinant DNA procedures or conventional biochemical methods. These drugs are packaged in completely sterile conditions, and scrupulous attention must be paid to maintaining complete cleanliness in the environment where the drugs and bottles and related paraphernalia are handled.

For example, quality control inspectors must be on guard where interferon is made. Small bottles containing the drug roll down a conveyor belt, and there must be constant surveillance of the line. Even the slightest defect in any of the bottles could lead to contamination. Quality control personnel rely on constant attention and surveillance and on efficient equipment maintained in excellent condition to continually monitor the integrity of the bottles.

Clinical Researchers

The pharmaceutical industry is home for the majority of biotechnologists involved in clinical research. Firms start negotiating with the U.S. Food and Drug Administration (FDA) as soon as new drugs are "born" in research and development departments. The FDA mandates a prescribed series of tests to be run by private industry and reviewed by the governmental agency. The process can last for as many as ten years before the FDA grants permission for the drugs to be sold in the United States. Clinical research specialists in industry are dedicated to developing, administrating, and analyzing the results of these clinical trials.

Regulatory Affairs

In the United States, federal and state governmental rules and regulations from a number of entities like the U.S. Food and Drug Administration and the Environmental Protection Agency (EPA) have fostered the need for biotechnologists trained in the area of regulatory affairs. In Canada, the Departments of the Ministry of Agriculture and the Ministry of Environment, as well as other agencies at the national and provincial levels, are responsible for similar areas of regulation. The industry needs a whole series of people ranging from lawyers to scientists whose job it is to understand what the governmental regulations are, what must be done to gain approval for a particular product, and how that is to be accomplished.

In addition, the government also employs biotechnologists in a variety of capacities, including being responsible for communicating the government's positions to industry, setting testing standards, and generally making sure that things are done properly and according to the standards and laws that apply.

Manufacturing

The next step after governmental approval of drugs or other biotechnology products is what is known in the industry as "scale-up"—turning something that was created in small quantities into what now will become a mass-produced item. Biotechnologists are needed to fill a variety of roles in the manufacturing/production sector. Manufacturing personnel usually will have a B.S. degree and/or work experience in engineering.

Daily Activities in the Lab

It is useful to know the broad range of activities that today's biotechnologists can pursue, but most action in the field still takes place in the research laboratories. Because most of the current job opportunities are in research, the following is a description of some of the day-to-day tasks in a laboratory.

Plan on putting in a full day's work daily no matter what your job title is. When, for example, lab assistants enter the laboratory in the morning, they address their attention to the simple gels they prepared the previous day. The lab assistants will photograph them and see what the analysis is.

They also will ask for work assignments from a postdoctoral scientist, scientist I, or research associate—for example, continuing to process tissue culture cells or bacteria or making DNA from bacteria cultures, which involves spinning the cultures down and making simple manipulations to isolate DNA from the cells. By the end of the day, lab assistants could be doing some simple digestions of DNA and might also be starting the gels for the next day.

The first thing research associates do when they check into work is to determine what the lab assistants are doing and what jobs should be assigned to them. For example, research associates might be putting a library of clones (a set of cloned DNA fragments) down onto filters and transferring them with the help of lab assistants.

The postdoctoral research scientist does bench work in the laboratory, along with extensive computer work and analysis, and writes papers.

As a rule of thumb, the higher the level a person attains in biotechnology, the less time he or she will spend at the lab workbench and the more time he or she will spend doing the administration tasks of managing projects and teams.

Some biotechnologists definitely want to move upward. At the lower levels of the industry, this frequently means earning advanced academic degrees. Many firms will pay for this education or for part of it.

Some individuals have no interest in the more prestigious job titles. Some do not want the more demanding responsibilities that come with advancement, and some do not want to give up the laboratory work to replace it with the tasks of management.

Entry-level positions sometimes draw persons with bachelor's degrees who may or may not know what they want to do with themselves professionally. Often this includes individuals who plan on going on to medical school in one to two years.

Jobs in Research Organizations and Corporations

Companies engaged in biotechnology-related research and development vary in the positions they offer, the education and experience required for similar positions, and the responsibilities of the staff at particular job levels. The job categories listed below give a general idea of the scope of positions existing within the industry.

Research and Development
Laboratory assistant
Research associate
Plant breeder

Quality Control
Quality-control analyst
Quality-control engineer

Health/safety specialist
Quality-assurance auditor
Validation engineer
Validation technician

Clinical Research
Clinical data operator
Clinical programmer analyst
Clinical data specialist
Clinical research associate
Animal technician
Technical writer

Regulatory Affairs
Regulatory affairs specialist
Coordinator/processor
Documentation specialist

Information Systems
Programmer analyst
Network architect

Marketing and Sales
Market research analyst
Sales representative
Technical services representative

Manufacturing and Production
Process development engineer
Production planner/scheduler

Manufacturing technician
Packaging/distribution handler
Manufacturing associate
Instrument/calibration technician
Process development associate

Nonscientific Biotechnology Careers

Many interesting and rewarding jobs in the field of biotechnology are nonscientific jobs. In the past, most work being done in the field of biotechnology took place in laboratories; now the scope of biotechnology has become so broad that there is a need for many types of professionals.

As with most other fields of interest, it takes a variety of disciplines to support the many sectors of the industry. As the field of biotechnology matures, the demand is expected to increase for skilled business managers, marketing personnel, salespeople, lawyers, regulatory specialists, financial analysts, professors, public relations personnel, and others who will be familiar with the skills, principles, and processes of biotechnology and who will support the scientific work with their own highly developed skills in related areas.

Many of these related job areas are even newer than the field of biotechnology. The educational underpinnings that prepare people for these pursuits are also in their infancy, but development of specific curricula, including interdisciplinary courses and majors, has been increasing rapidly.

You can learn more about these career possibilities through your own research, by speaking with contacts you have made in the field, by attending career fairs and professional conferences, and by studying the websites of the multitude of biotechnology associations (see Appendixes B and C) that exist today. Almost every association website provides links for additional career and/or employment information, and their newsletters list employment opportunities and ads that include job descriptions, as well.

4

EDUCATIONAL PREPARATION

THE EDUCATIONAL ROUTES to a career in biotechnology are as varied as its scope. Because biotechnology is an interdisciplinary field in which the knowledge and skills of many academic disciplines converge and blend, and because it is so extraordinarily diverse, there are many recommended ways to prepare for a career in this area.

Majors and Interdisciplinary Emphases in Biotechnology

There is a growing roster of schools with specifically designated biotechnology majors at the undergraduate and graduate levels, as well as additional schools with substantial programs blending courses from different departments that are specifically geared to training biotechnologists. Universities and schools with respected traditional majors in the life sciences, organic chemistry, and the computer sciences also provide a good foundation for specialization in biotechnological knowledge.

An extensive list of colleges and universities offering majors or emphases in one or more areas of biotechnology as of 2006 and, in many cases, having outstanding research centers and other distinctions, is provided in Appendix D. Annotations and websites are included.

Specific course listings are subject to frequent change as new classes are added, so you will need to look at the most current school catalog when you are making your plans. You may also want to talk with representatives of potential employers in the field to ascertain what training they prefer their employees to have.

Many academics and industry observers believe that the best preparation for biotechnology is training in a traditional discipline, such as genetics or plant physiology, while also learning specific disciplines of biotechnology. Individuals with such backgrounds can work on interdisciplinary teams and focus on specific problems for which they are best qualified.

Dr. David Pramer, former director of the Waksman Institute of Microbiology at Rutgers University, has stated:

> It would be unwise for universities to offer educational programs in biotechnology that are narrowly conceived or overly professional, and it is essential for university scientists within traditional academic disciplines not to abdicate a responsibility to educate biotechnologists. . . . To continue to flourish, biotechnology must be nourished by a steady supply of individuals who also are well educated in traditional disciplines. Since biotechnology five years from now may be quite different from what it is today, the key to educating a biotechnologist is flexibility in specialized aspects of a program that is firmly based in science and engineering.

Of necessity, many biotechnology firms require a diversity of scientific skills because of the broad range of applications in this field. A solid background in the life sciences is necessary for virtually all positions. Disciplines in high demand include the following.

Agricultural sciences
Biochemical engineering
Biochemistry
Biology
Botany
Chemistry
Computer science
Enzymology
Genetics
Immunology
Microbiology
Molecular biology
Mycology
Veterinary medicine
Virology
Zoology

Growth and Changes in Biotechnology Education

College and university programs have been expanded to keep up with the educational and research demands of the emerging biotechnology industry, and new programs are also being added. Current programs include two-year (associate) degree programs, four-year degree programs, graduate degree programs, and short professional-level courses and seminars for scientists concentrating in particular biotechnology areas.

Important educational experiences are also provided by research centers based in universities. While these centers generally do not sponsor courses or grant degrees, they do enhance biotechnology education on their campuses. They offer access to equipment, faculty development, and research opportunities for both graduates and undergraduates. These centers also often provide a forum for discussions of education and training and help to propose, test, and establish new directions of education.

Some university programs have been developed with direct coordination with the program developers at other schools, so that you may find complementary emphases in a cluster of schools, especially where one or more community colleges may support their students in preparation for transfer to particular four-year schools later. Others have been developed relatively independently of the course offerings in other institutions. However, most schools do faithfully keep up with national and international trends in education and research in this field, and most also have interaction with industry. Contacts with industry may include surveying local biotechnology companies and discussing program proposals and directions of projects, as well as the kinds of specialists the companies expect to be hiring in the foreseeable future.

A Young Curriculum

With the exception of programs in biochemical engineering, most biotechnology programs are relatively new. The oldest began about 1980. Many more were developed or expanded in the 1980s and 1990s, and new programs have been appearing ever since 2000.

A large number of biotechnology programs were first set up in 1983. This indicates a two-year lag from 1981, the year that many of the first biotechnology companies were founded. Two years is a relatively short time to develop curricula and approve programs. Some institutions moved quickly into biotechnology at that time. Others formed their programs later in the 1980s and the 1990s. Each year a number of new ones were started. They were aimed at a variety of educational levels. At the doctoral level, many programs were established in bioprocessing and biochemical engineering. Traditional Ph.D. programs in molecular biology, microbiology, biochemistry, and others also support the biotechnology industry.

Changes from Early Curricula

The first biotechnology programs often were formed around a core of recombinant DNA technology. Commonly taught courses and skills included tissue culturing, hybridoma technology, immunochemistry, bioprocess engineering, fermentation, and purification and separation sciences.

Training in bioprocess engineering has expanded in recent years and is available in some schools through the chemical engineering departments.

The majority of the undergraduate chemical engineering curriculum is mandated by the accreditation standards of the American Institute of Chemical Engineers and the Accreditation Board for Engineering and Technology. In some universities, students interested in biochemical engineering can use their electives for courses in biochemistry, microbiology, biochemical engineering, genetics, and biology.

Training programs tend to be laboratory-intensive, except for short courses and workshops. Academic program directors have routinely found that industry requires hands-on laboratory experience and have designed their programs accordingly.

Associate Degree Programs

The need for biotechnicians with specialized training has prompted a number of community colleges to institute biotechnology training programs. Early in the development of biotechnology, most work was done by highly educated, innovative thinkers, who often had to develop new procedures as their research progressed. As with all technologies, as biotechnology matured, more of the work has become routine and some of it can be assigned to less highly trained technicians for whom a two-year training program may be appropriate.

Associate of applied sciences (A.A.S.) programs in biotechnology are taught primarily at community or junior colleges. These programs are designed to fill the need for biotechnicians, similar to the more established need of chemical technicians, although students from these programs may go on to four-year colleges.

The need for biotechnicians at the A.A.S. level has increased in recent years, but a huge need for personnel trained at this level has not yet emerged, perhaps partly as a reflection of the general state of the overall economy and job market, but there are also other factors in industry, including the following.

1. Training demands for technicians in biotechnology currently differ from those for technicians in other technology fields most significantly in that they require a broader and more interdisciplinary technical base.

2. Many biotechnology companies prefer biotechnicians to have at least a bachelor's degree.

3. The biotechnology industry's present need for employment of biotechnicians from two-year training programs is not large enough to justify the expense of starting new programs at many two-year institutions.

4. Two-year programs hold most potential in areas with the largest markets for biotechnicians, including California, Maryland, Massachusetts, New Jersey, New York, and Seattle. The need for biotechnicians is growing in other parts of the country and will likely expand in some states as the biotechnology industry bases grow.

Some industry officials have not been supportive of the two-year programs thus far. Concerns have included whether two years in college can provide the knowledge necessary to manage complex instrumentation and sensitive organisms and that technicians without a more substantial theoretical understanding may not be able to adapt to the ever-changing needs of a rapidly evolving technology. Industry representatives have also given these reasons for skepticism: at times there has been an oversupply of biologists with B.S. and M.S. degrees available for technician work, two-year programs lack the breadth and depth of four-year programs, and companies need the research background provided by B.S. and M.S. programs.

Small companies are more likely to require employees to assume multiple duties, some of which will require more training than two-year programs provide.

As dedicated biotechnology companies have grown and matured, some reasons for reluctance in hiring graduates of two-year programs have dissipated. As a company's overall workload and staff increase, it can divide tasks by level of skill and may want to employ more people full-time at the lower skill levels. Also, as work continues to shift from research and development to production, more routine tasks will have to be done. Larger companies may also be able to afford more time for on-the-job training if that is needed.

Two-Year A.A.S. Program

The two-year or technician-level program usually leads to the A.A.S. degree in a science or biotechnology area, although some programs are also designed as certificate programs. Programs for preparation in the following areas are common:

- Bioinformatics
- Clinical laboratory technician
- Laboratory animal technician
- Biotechnology laboratory technician
- Electron microscopy technician

These programs prepare students to work in laboratories or supporting areas, in research and development laboratories, or in small-scale production facilities. Students acquire skills and knowledge in such areas as documentation, instrumentation, chromatography, microbiology, fermentation technology, cell culturing, protein purification methods, and recombinant DNA methodologies. The students' experience usually includes serving as interns in a local laboratory.

Prerequisites for admission to this program include an interest in science; a minimum of previous completion of high school classes in biology, chemistry, and algebra (or the equivalent); and completion of a high school diploma or GED.

The four-semester, two-year associate program typically includes thirty to forty credits of program courses: twelve to fifteen credits of science support courses, twelve to fifteen credits of general education courses, and six to ten credits of elective courses. Laboratory courses are sometimes offered in cooperation with nearby commercial and research center laboratories, and these provide additional credit options.

Bachelor's and Graduate-Level Programs

Numerous colleges and universities have instituted bachelor's-level programs in biotechnology. These programs emphasize hands-on laboratory experience but include substantial theoretical science and humanities courses. Students are prepared either to go directly to work in industrial labs or to enter master's or doctoral programs.

The bachelor of science degree in biotechnology often represents an interdepartmental program emphasizing the molecular basis of life processes and the techniques utilized to study and control these processes. Students can usually take an integrated sequence of courses selected from the curricula of the departments of biology, chemistry, computer science, engineering, physics, animal and food sciences, and plant and earth sciences.

In some colleges and universities the B.S. degree in biotechnology is offered in the college of arts and sciences; in some it is available through the colleges of agriculture, chemistry, engineering, or other related areas. Programs are often combined with the colleges' or universities' strongest scientific offerings; for example, a school famous for its college of agriculture will offer a biotechnology degree related to that area, or a school with a famous oceanography research center can be expected to offer a biotechnology major in relation to marine biology.

Curriculum Examples

Because programs will vary, it is useful to examine more than one school's curriculum. A few examples will illustrate the variety and range of programs being offered in the United States and Canada.

College of Arts and Sciences

The biotechnology curriculum at a typical liberal arts college might progress as follows.

First Year—Fall
Calculus
Freshman English I
General Chemistry I
General Chemistry Lab I
Introduction to Biology
Physical Education

First Year—Spring
Freshman English II
General Chemistry II
General Chemistry Lab II
General Education—Fine Arts
General Education—Social and Behavioral Sciences
Health and Fitness

Second Year—Fall
General Botany or General Zoology
General Physics
General Physics Lab
Modern Language

Organic Chemistry I
Organic Chemistry Lab I

Second Year—Spring
Cell Biology
General Education—Literature
General Physics
General Physics Lab
Organic Chemistry II
Organic Chemistry Lab II
Physical Education

Third Year—Fall
Analytical Chemistry
Analytical Chemistry Lab
Bacteriology
Biochemistry I
General Education—Social and Behavioral Sciences

Third Year—Spring
Animal Cell Culture
Biochemistry II
Biochemistry Lab
Biotechnology elective
Genetics and Evolution
Plant Tissue Culture: Theory and Practice

Fourth Year—Fall
Bioethics
Biotech elective
Food Microbiology

Molecular Biology
Virology

Fourth Year—Spring
Biotechnology elective
Biotechnology seminar
General Education—Liberal Arts
General elective
Humanities
Social Science

Technical Institute

At this large school, students who pursue a bachelor's degree in biology may choose a biotechnology track from among several specialty tracks. Along with a full slate of courses required for biology majors, they complete twenty-one to twenty-four credit hours in the following areas of microbial biotechnology and microbiology.

Fermentation Lab
Industrial Microbiology
Medical Bacteriology
Microbial Ecology
Microbial Genetics
Microbial Genetics Lab
Microbial Physiology
Microbial Physiology Lab

Liberal Arts University

The department of biology at this university offers an undergraduate certificate in biotechnology as part of its B.A. and B.S. degrees in biology, along with a similar certificate as part of its M.S. and Ph.D. degrees in biology.

At the bachelor's degree level, students may obtain an undergraduate certificate in biotechnology by completing specified courses along with those required for the B.S. in biology program.

Biotechnology courses, some of which are required and some of which are elective, include:

Advanced Biochemistry
Biological Chemistry Laboratory
Gene Expression in Eukaryotes
Gene Expression in Prokaryotes
Genetics Laboratory
Immunobiology
Introduction to Biotechnology
Microbiology
Microbiology Laboratory
Molecular Cell Biology
Techniques in Molecular Biology
Topics in Biological Chemistry
Virology

The graduate certificate can be earned independently or in conjunction with a master's or doctoral degree in biology. It consists of an eighteen-credit-hour program, with available internships, and includes courses in the following areas:

Biochemistry elective
Cell biology elective
Gene Expression in Eukaryotes
Gene Expression in Prokaryotes

Immunology elective
Techniques in Molecular Biology

Master's degree programs in biotechnology are multidisciplinary and often interdepartmental. Many programs preparing students for careers in bioprocessing are at the master's and doctoral levels, since most people in the industry consider M.S. and Ph.D. degrees to be entry-level requirements for bioprocessing jobs.

Doctoral degrees are required for the most advanced positions. Following are examples of programs offered at the graduate level.

Canadian University

This major university offers a short-term graduate certificate in biotechnology, which is designed for students who already hold a four-year degree in the biological or medical sciences and who want additional background to prepare for jobs in the biotechnology industry.

The certificate program may be completed in four months. Students gain hands-on laboratory experience based on the latest molecular biology techniques. They may also benefit from a biotechnology management course, which provides information on how the biotechnology industry works. Some students also participate in a twelve-week practicum involving placement in a biotechnology company.

University Near a Major Biotechnology Hub

This school offers a master's of biotechnology program with a cross-disciplinary approach. Students prepare for careers in the biotechnology and pharmaceutical industries. Students can choose from three program tracks.

Basic Biotechnology

This track emphasizes basic molecular biology. Students complete eleven computational courses consisting of six core courses and five courses from their chosen track. Core curriculum courses in the basic biotechnology track include:

Biochemistry

Biotechnology I, a course covering molecular biology, recombinant DNA technology, transgenic organisms, protein engineering, combinatorial chemistry, and molecular modeling

Biotechnology II: Engineering Biotechnology, covering production of biological molecules using cell culture technologies. This course includes an introduction to bioreactor design and control, molecular and cellular bioseparations, and tissue and cellular engineering.

Laboratory in Biotechnology and Genetic Engineering Statistics

Biotechnology Seminar I and II, providing an overview of current scientific, regulatory, and ethical issues in biotechnology. Topics include drug discovery, elements of pharmaceutical patent law, design of clinical trials, FDA approval process, developments in computational biology, practical aspects of clinical pharmacology, and contemporary issues in bioethics.

Other courses in this track include:

Advanced Cell Biology
Advanced Developmental Biology
Current Topics in Plant Molecular Biology
Experimental Principles in Molecular Biology
Genetic Systems
Immunobiology
Mammalian Developmental Biology
Molecular Genetics
Prokaryotic Molecular Genetics
Thesis research (two terms of independent study are
    required)

Engineering Biotechnology

This track stresses bioprocess engineering central to pharmaceutical manufacturing. Courses include:

Pharmaceutical Manufacturing, which is a continuation of
    Biotechnology II and covers production of biological
    molecules, bioreactors, bioseparations, and tissue and
    cellular engineering
Advanced Cell Biology
Biomaterials
Biomedical Instrumentation
Biochemistry
Cell Biology and Molecular Structure
Cellular Bioengineering
Computational Biology
Foundations of Engineering Mathematics I and II
Fundamentals of Pharmacology

Interfacial Bioscience
Mechanics of Biomaterials
Molecular Biophysics
Molecular Genetics
Pharmaceutical Manufacturing
Quantitative Human Physiology
Transport Processes I and II

Computational Biology/Bioinformatics

This track prepares students for analysis of expanding genomic databases. Courses include:

Algorithms
Computational Biology (two courses)
Databases, Advanced Databases
Programming Languages
Statistics II

University and Health Center

This program is offered by a university and a health research center that have combined their scientific faculties and their research and educational facilities in order to offer a graduate program in biotechnology.

The program allows students to acquire knowledge and skills in biotechnology along with an academic background in biochemistry for an M.S. degree in biotechnology.

Students take eighteen credit hours of required courses providing background in biochemistry, molecular biology, and theoretical applications of biotechnology, along with six elective credit hours and twelve research hours, including a thesis research project.

Core lecture courses use televideo conferencing equipment so students can attend classes at either of the participating campuses. The lecture approach is combined with hands-on laboratory experiences in areas such as the following:

Amino Acid Sequencing
Applications of Immunology
Basic Biotech Laboratory Procedures
DNA Sequencing
Fermentation Technology
Gene Expression
Gene Manipulation and Modification
Molecular Genetics
PCR Technology
Protein Biochemistry
Protein Synthesis and Purification

Research Centers

University-based biotechnology research centers take many forms. The purposes of the centers frequently include conducting or sponsoring research, coordinating biotechnology research and training among the various university departments, providing a forum for multidisciplinary projects, and purchasing specialized equipment. Centers may also be involved with local biotechnology companies in technology transfer and economic development activities. Some centers sponsor seminars, workshops, and short courses for both academic and industrial scientists. Examples include:

Northwestern University
Center for Biotechnology
Evanston, IL 60201
www.northwestern.edu

University of Colorado
Colorado Institute of Research in Biotechnology
Ft. Collins, CO 80523
www.natsci.colostate.edu

University of Illinois
Biotechnology Center
Urbana, IL 61820
www.research.uiuc.edu

University of Maryland
Biotechnology Institute
Rockville, MD 20850
www.umbi.umd.edu

Virginia Polytechnic Institute and State University
Fralin Biotechnology Center
Blacksburg, VA 24061
www.biotech.vt.edu

Canadian institutions with biotechnology centers include the following:

Dalhousie University
Department of Oceanography
Halifax, NS
Canada B3H 4H6
www.dal.ca

McGill University
Montreal, QC
Canada H3A 2T5
www.mcgill.ca

University of British Columbia
2329 West Mall
Vancouver, BC
Canada V6T 1Z2
www.ubc.ca

University of Calgary
2500 University Drive NW
Calgary, AB
Canada T2N 1N4
www.ucalgary.ca

University of Montreal
Montreal, QC
Canada H3C 3J7
www.umontreal.ca

University of Toronto
Toronto, ON
Canada M5S 1A1
www.utoronto.ca

For more information about available programs, contact the state
Coordinating Council for Higher Education for any state in which
you are interested, or contact schools directly and obtain catalogs
of course offerings (see Appendix D). It is important to contact

each school in which you may be interested when you are getting ready to make your decisions to be sure you have the latest and most up-to-date information.

Continuing Education

Continuing education has emerged as a significant need, given the rapid development of new biotechniques and the large number of researchers who received their formal training before new techniques were widely integrated into biological research. Short courses like those described previously are a principal way of accomplishing this need for continuing education.

In addition, a formal process for continuing education units of credit (CEUs) has been established. Colleges and universities sponsor special CEU events, and national association conferences and other events offer continuing education credits for participation in some workshops and seminars.

Most biotechnology companies provide in-house courses and training funds for their employees' continuing education. Continuing education is an integral part of many companies' day-to-day operations. Companies hold seminars, sponsor cross-departmental training, and establish systems to keep their research staffs abreast of current research and market trends.

Continuing education is a principal motivation for companies to enter into collaborative arrangements with universities. One of the advantages of these arrangements is that they frequently allow company scientists to spend time in university laboratories updating their skills.

Staying Informed

The field of biotechnology is one in which professionals will continue to learn throughout their careers. Internet and print newsletters, scholarly papers and books, academic and trade journals, membership in professional associations, attendance at regional meetings, and national and international conferences are among the many ways of keeping up with the field. You will want to take advantage of these to ensure that your awareness of the progress of your industry is continually maintained at a professional level.

5

Employment Opportunities

The number of jobs in the biosciences in the United States has been growing in recent years. While employment opportunities in biotechnology were somewhat stagnant as a result of the economic downturn from 2000 to 2002, forecasts predict that the outlook will be improved through the year 2014. Industry reports for 2005 and 2006 indicated an upturn and, based upon investment, research, new products in the pipeline, and plans for expansion in general, hiring growth was expected to continue. According to the Biotechnology Industry Organization (BIO), although the total U.S. employment declined by 0.7 percent from 2000 through 2005, biotechnology employment gained by slightly more than 1 percent.

The industry report by Ernst & Young in 2006 stated that U.S. employment in the biosciences in 2004 had reached 1.2 million, with employment found to be in all fifty states, the District of Columbia, and Puerto Rico. In Canada, industry reports for biotechnology are included in the professional, scientific, and technical services sector, which showed 2004 total employment of 667,573, up from 641,304 in 2001.

In the United States, approximately two-thirds of the jobs were in medical research and equipment, with the total divided between four sectors. Distribution of the jobs was as follows:

1. Research, testing, and medical laboratories, which employed 33 percent
2. Medical devices and equipment, which employed 33 percent
3. Drugs and pharmaceuticals, which employed 25 percent
4. Agricultural feedstock and chemicals, which employed 8 percent

States and territories showed strength in various sectors, as indicated in Table 5.1.

In Canada the highest employment sectors were in agricultural feedstock and chemicals and in drugs and pharmaceuticals. Areas with highest employment levels were British Columbia, Alberta, Ontario, and Quebec, and there was significant development in other provinces, as well.

Table 5.1 Highest Employment Areas for Biotechnology Jobs

Sector	Highest Employment
Agricultural feedstocks and chemicals	Florida, Illinois, Iowa, Ohio, Texas
Drugs and pharmaceuticals	Illinois, Indiana, New York, New Jersey, Pennsylvania, Puerto Rico
Medical devices and equipment	California, Florida, Massachusetts, Minnesota, New York
Research, testing, and medical laboratories	California, Massachusetts, New Jersey, New York

According to statistics from the U.S. Department of Labor, by 2004 in the United States, both the medical research and the pharmaceutical sectors showed an increase in the numbers of people employed over those of 2001, but the agricultural and equipment sectors showed slight declines in overall employment.

Biotechnology employment in the United States varies greatly by state and by sector of the industry. Because federal research funds had declined following the economic downturn of 2001, some states and some of the largest cities have undertaken major initiatives in supporting the development of biotechnology industry in their areas. They have done this by creating cooperative relationships with university and medical research programs, other state and local governments, and private industry. In some areas, these special educational efforts begin with high school programs that feed directly into community college, college, and university programs, and also into private industry.

Biotechnology employment prospects can be found for recent graduates with degrees ranging from a high school diploma to a Ph.D. Openings exist for graduates with backgrounds in almost all areas of life science, particularly biology, genetics, molecular biology, biochemistry, microbiology, cell biology, and animal or plant biology. An increasing number of biotechnology positions also are becoming available for chemists and chemical engineers, physicists, engineers, and computer information scientists. As new products such as medicines, agrochemicals, and animal health drugs are being created and tested for approval by the FDA, more specialists such as doctors, veterinarians, ecologists, pharmacologists, and toxicologists are needed to assess product safety. The expansion of the industry is also creating opportunities for people trained in management, marketing, sales, finance, statistics, and information processing.

Industry Facts and Trends

Because biotechnology has received extensive coverage in the press, it is easy to forget that the field is actually still in its early stages. In the 1970s, biotechnology was barely an industry at all, largely unheard of by most people. By the 1980s, it had grown into a $2 billion market. By the end of the 1990s, biotechnology had mushroomed. In 1998, $97 billion had been invested in the U.S. industry, and by April 2005, this number had swelled to a market value of more than $311 billion.

According to the Biotechnology Industry Organization, the United States is currently the world leader in biotechnology product research, development, and commercialization. Biotechnology products that are already on the market include lifesaving health care goods, superproducing farm crops, and microbial pesticides. Recent biotechnological advances are soon expected to offer many healthier foods, more disease- and insect-resistant crops, new energy sources, more efficient environmental cleanup techniques, and individually customized suites of medicines.

U.S. Biotechnology Companies

On New Year's Day 2004, there were 1,473 biotechnology companies in the United States, and 314 of those were publicly held, according to the Biotechnology Industry Organization. Many of the corporate names will be familiar to you, but new ones are appearing with remarkable speed. You'll want to follow this development and become aware of the important players in the field.

Leaders in various industry segments and in various parts of the country can be readily identified if you check industry organization websites and look at the "Events" listings. For most events—conventions, seminars, conferences, and workshops—a program will be posted. If you examine the program schedule, with presentations and speakers listed, you'll find a representation of the leadership in that area.

For example, at conferences, companies sponsor "Presenters" who give slides shows or speeches in their special areas. The event's program lists them by category, so it is easy to learn who took an active part in meetings and which organizations and corporations are investing in their future in any given area.

It costs money to send employees to trade shows and conventions, so if a university, corporation, or other organization is presenting at a meeting, it means that it has a substantial interest in the topic of the meeting, and it also has a stake in it for its own future. Let's look at the names of some of the presenters at a conference about investment in the industry. If organizations are involved in the financial end of these issues, they are planning to grow in these areas. If they are successful, that also means they will be hiring. The presenters' names are listed by the category of biotechnology product or service in which they are involved.

Food
Tufts University

Instrumentation
British Columbia Institute of Technology
Flexpoint Sensor Systems
National University of Singapore
University of Vermont

Health Care and Medical Devices
Boston University
Gestion Univalor, Limited Partnership

International Science and Technology Center
Maine Medical Center Research Institute
Rice University
Tufts University
University of Vermont
WVHTC Foundation
Yale University

Pharmaceuticals and Biotechnology
BIOHemaCell
Boston Biomedical Research Institute
Boston University
Inova Unicamp Innovation Agency
Phoqus Pharmaceuticals
Rensselaer Polytechnic
Rice University
Stockholm University
Tufts University
Unicamp Innovation Agency
University of California San Diego
University of Michigan
University of Vermont
WVHTC Foundation

Personal Care
Harvard University

Software and Services
Amphion Innovations
Swiss Federal Institute of Technology

University of Alaska–Fairbanks
University of Massachusetts–Lowell

From these listings you can see the variety of areas these organizations are interested in. Some are involved in more than one area. If they get new funding or make new partnerships or other agreements as a result of the meeting, these organizations will be starting up some new projects. And new projects usually mean new jobs.

Canadian Biotechnology Companies

Canadian corporations are also growing rapidly, and a small sampling of some outstanding names includes:

Oncology Therapeutics
Biomira, Inc.
GeminX Biotechnologies, Inc.

Eye, Spinal Cord, and Joint Therapeutics
iCo Therapeutics

Apopotois Control Drugs
Aegera, Inc.

Agricultural, Environmental, Industrial, Energy, Bioprocessing, Health, and Nutrition Applications
Ag-West BIO, Inc.

Cosmetics, Pharmaceuticals, Chemicals, and Nutrition
Atrium Biotechnologies, Inc.

More information about Canadian companies can be acquired by contacting the Ministries of Agriculture, Health, and the Environment, each of which have many individual departments that govern the activities of various segments of the biotechnology industry in Canada. Information on jobs can also be accessed by going to the Canada Biotechnology Human Resource Council, which publishes "The Petri Dish," a job portal that provides up-to-date job postings, a résumé database, and career information. It can be accessed at www.bhrc.ca/career.

Getting Information About Organizations

When you see something that interests you, you can easily follow up in your career research. Go to the website of the organization that looks active in the area you want to find out more about. Most often the website will provide a link for jobs, careers, employment, or a similar label. By researching the website further, you'll also find out more about the organization and its history and management structure. You can also go to the website of the professional association for that area and check the membership listings to find related organizations.

To supplement your own research, see a reference librarian at a public or university library for more information. Ask for the industry directory for the organization you are interested in. The directory will give more specific information, such as the organization's financial history, number of products produced in recent years, the number of employees or, if the organization is a school, the number of graduates. The website will give indications of the organization's success in its field, such as awards, alliance partnerships, history of ownership, and many other items that will help you decide if this is a strong or a weak organization and whether it is worth your while to apply there, either as a place of education or as an employer.

Certain geographical regions, cities, and states have a high concentration of biotechnology research organizations and manufacturing and production companies. Sometimes they are referred to as biotechnology hubs. The largest are:

Los Angeles/Orange County
Michigan/Ann Arbor
Mid-Atlantic/Delaware, Maryland
New England
New Jersey
New York
North Carolina
Philadelphia/Delaware Valley
San Diego
San Francisco Bay
Seattle
Texas
Madison, Wisconsin

Current Employment

According to the U.S. Department of Labor, in 2004 there were more than 138,000 people employed in the biotechnology industry, of which about 77,000 were biological scientists. In this industry in general, the working conditions, salaries and wages, and opportunities for advancement are better than average. Because so many biotechnology companies are small and relatively new, some of them offer excellent incentive compensation plans in place of high salaries.

Biopharmaceutical Outlook

According to industry experts, the outlook for the biopharmaceutical industry in 2006 was robust, and its growth was accelerating. The markets for human health care products held increasing potential for both prescription and other products. Some of the strongest growth areas are agri-bio projects, animal health and growth, aquaculture, new health-related biomaterials, and personalized nutrition. Against this background of expansion, jobs in the biotechnology sector were predicted to grow steadily, slightly faster than average, through the year 2014.

Agricultural Outlook

New biotechnological products are making enormous changes in many agricultural industries, and many more are being developed and are close to being put into production. Some of the products that have attracted public attention are clones, fluorescent Glo-fish, the Enviropig that has lower-phosphorous wastes, double-muscled poultry that has more meat, cattle that are resistant to mad cow disease, and, in fish farming, genetically engineered salmon that are larger and more profitable to market.

John C. Matheson, III, FDA Center for Veterinary Medicine, Rockville, Maryland, spoke to the USDA Agricultural Outlook Forum of 2006 about animal biotech products. He said that genetic engineering of animals is available to small and large companies and laboratories all over the world and, if a product is profitable, it will be put to use. Public controversy and governmental scrutiny and regulations will test products and will cause some to be discontinued if they prove unsafe or unpopular enough to reduce their profitability, but genetic engineering of animals is here to stay. He said, too, that in some cases it provides an alternative to the use of antibiotics and steroid hormones in animals and feed.

In the area of animal genetic engineering, future employment growth is not certain due to the possible effects of public acceptance of products and the possibility of new regulation of applications and testing. But it is expected, as a part of the overall biotechnology industry, to increase as fast or faster than average through 2014.

Sales and Revenues

Sales of U.S. biotechnology products are growing and had $46 billion in revenues in 2004. Biotechnology companies in the United States are currently selling their products in many parts of the world, including Canada, China, Eastern Europe, Japan, Latin America, the Pacific Rim, Russia, and Western Europe.

Employment and Income

According to a spokesperson for the Biotechnology Industry Organization, the median annual salary in the industry in 2006 was $65,000, and this included entry-level and experienced workers.

According to the U.S. Department of Labor's *Occupational Outlook Handbook, 2006–2007*, general biological scientists in nonsupervisory, supervisory, and managerial positions in the federal government in 2005 earned an average salary of $69,908. Average salaries for specialists such as botanists were $62,207; ecologists, $72,021; microbiologists, $80,798; geneticists, $85,170; physiologists, $93,208; and zoologists, $101,601.

Nationally, biochemists and biophysicists earned a median salary of $68,950 in May 2004, with the middle 50 percent earning between $49,430 and $88,540. The lowest 10 percent earned less than $38,710, and the highest 10 percent earned more than $110,660. Median annual earnings of microbiologists were $54,840 in May 2004, with the middle 50 percent earning between $41,000 and $74,260. The lowest 10 percent earned less than $32,630, and the highest 10 percent earned more than $101,720. Median annual earnings of zoologists and wildlife biologists were $50,330 in May 2004, with the middle 50 percent earning between $39,150 and $63,800. The lowest 10 percent earned less than $31,450, and the highest 10 percent earned more than $81,200. Median annual earnings of biochemists and biophysicists employed in scientific research and development services were $73,900 in May 2004.

According to the National Association of Colleges and Employers, beginning salary offers in July 2005 averaged $31,258 a year for bachelor's degree recipients in entry-level jobs in the biological and life sciences.

Salaries and benefits were highest, in general, in the most concentrated areas of biology and biotechnical research and production, such as in the Boston, Baltimore/Washington DC, Seattle, San Francisco, Los Angeles/San Diego, and other "hub" areas. In general, salaries and benefits in smaller towns, in less concentrated or relatively isolated job markets, especially in the Midwest and the South, were lower, although there were notable exceptions, particularly in certain universities and research centers.

Salaries are affected by a number of factors, some of which are under the individual's control and some of which are strictly external, such as those listed below.

- Educational background
- Skill and experience
- Geographical location

- Size and type of employer
- Level of responsibility
- Previous or existing salary
- Competition for employees
- Competition for jobs
- Benefits

Most employers provide a variety of benefits to employees in addition to salaries, including some or all of the following:

- Dental insurance
- Disability insurance
- Holidays
- Life insurance
- Medical insurance
- Personal time
- Retirement plans, 401(k)
- Sick time
- Stock options and/or profit sharing
- Tuition assistance

Changing Personnel Needs

Recently the biotechnology industry has shifted much of its emphasis away from basic research, focusing on converting research findings into marketable products. This means that many companies are moving from the research and development phase into production and marketing.

Although there is still a need for research scientists, this industry shift has created an increasing number of job opportunities for production engineers, marketing specialists, human resource specialists, administrative assistants, public relations specialists, data-processing staff, accountants, programmers, and other business specialists.

Many companies, particularly mid-size and large firms, look for managers with a combination of business and technical backgrounds. For example, a person with a B.S. in the biological sciences and an M.B.A., or a person with an undergraduate business degree and a master's degree in environmental policy, would be very useful to companies developing agricultural or veterinary products. The composition of the biotechnological industry directly affects its job seekers.

Quite often small companies in biotechnology, many of them in the health care field, experience management difficulties and are "swallowed up" by larger corporations. If the consolidation movement continues, the industry's efforts may focus on new areas of biotechnology.

Stay aware of the changing faces of the subindustries that comprise biotechnology. Study the newspaper reports in scientific magazines, journals, and the financial press. Read the latest employment want ads. Your career preparation, based upon your realistic feel for the needs of the field today and tomorrow, will pay off for you.

Personnel shortages in certain emerging fields are for the most part unavoidable. This is due both to the difficulty of predicting which fields will have the heaviest demands and the lag time required for educational institutions to gear up for new fields. The expense of new faculty and new equipment prevents schools from rapidly moving into them. It frequently follows that in areas where there is a shortage of researchers, there also are not enough university instructors. For example, pharmaceutical companies are "plucking" x-ray crystallographers with skills in working with biological molecules off campuses at a rate that threatens to undercut both research and the training of future crystallographers.

In another example, a lack of microbial ecologists resulted from increased interest in the release of engineered organisms into the environment. The U.S. Environmental Protection Agency (EPA) pronounced some of the functions of microbial ecologists as priority areas. These areas included ecological risk assessment, ecosystem structure and workings, and ecological and toxicological effects. Until recently, microbial ecology was a relatively obscure field that attracted less money and talent than the more glamorous fields such as molecular biology.

In recent decades, protein chemistry has emerged as a high-need field. The knowledge of making, purifying, and stabilizing proteins to their active form is required, especially in pharmaceutical applications. The need for immunologists has increased, too, due to demand in both monoclonal antibody development and in AIDS research.

Whether shortages of bioprocess engineers actually materialize will depend on how rapidly biotechnology products are brought to the marketplace and how fast universities and their students respond to predicted personnel needs. While a shortage of bioprocess engineers would create a serious bottleneck for the industry, the actual number needed may not be that great. Bioprocess engineering does not demand a large workforce. It has been estimated that personnel requirements for bioprocessing, even after firms enter mass production, will represent only 10 to 15 percent of all those employed in biotechnology. Technological advances such as biosensors and computer-controlled continuous bioprocessing could reduce the need for bioprocess engineers.

Potential personnel shortages may also be eased somewhat by scientist mobility. It was thought at one time, for instance, that the supply of plant molecular biologists was running low. In fact, however, the field of plant molecular biology expanded at a rapid pace in more recent years due to the large pool of molecular biology postdoctoral fellows and trainees. While many of these scientists were specialists in animal or bacterial systems, they were able to apply their skills and knowledge of molecular genetics to plant systems. The postdoctoral pool thus served as a buffer, although the need remained for biotechnologists with plant expertise.

No such postdoctoral pool has traditionally existed for bioprocess engineering. The universities have responded with increased attention to bioprocess engineering.

Belief is widespread that interdisciplinary training should be increased, but opinions vary with regard to the specific disciplines that should be included. Industrialists have expressed needs for "life-science-oriented engineers and engineering-oriented life scientists," as well as "chemical engineers with an appreciation of biosynthesis" and "biologists with an understanding of production problems."

Different types of firms have different personnel needs. Generally smaller firms have a higher percentage of Ph.D. scientists than do larger ones. Small firms are more likely to be concentrating on relatively basic research and development. Small firms are also less likely to be involved in large-scale production and can, therefore, be expected to have less need for technicians than their larger counterparts. Some analysts have concluded that small firms are less able to afford on-the-job training. They need people who can get up to speed right away. Other experts find that employers are interested in persons with broad general education who are willing to teach special skills on the job.

In some markets, the job openings are there; in others the job market is tight due to the overall state of the economy. According to the Department of Labor, biotechnology job openings in general are expected to continue to be better than average through the year 2014, driven by growth in investment in biotechnology research and development and in the innovative products and services being produced.

6

SUCCEEDING ON THE JOB

THIS CHAPTER OUTLINES practical ways of thinking and the conduct that biotechnologists need to practice in the work world. Many of these skills and attitudes are applicable to scientists in all fields. Others are especially unique to a pioneer science that, quite frequently, expects its personnel to be flexible enough to master challenging and precedent-setting assignments that are not yet covered in textbooks.

If you can demonstrate a history of textbook learning and solid, on-the-job work performance, you will probably get the attention of a company's hiring specialist. Yet a job quest can be lost for you or any candidate who appears to be lacking other basic ingredients needed for productive participation in biotechnology.

At first you might think of these characteristics as vague, intangible, innate personality traits with which one is born. However, a good measure of self-awareness, good people skills, and the positive aptitudes and attitudes that make fellow employees and employers comfortable can be acquired and maintained. Know what these helpful behavioral characteristics are, and make them a part of the way you conduct yourself. For now, they can make the difference between a job offer and a job rejection. Later on, they can make the difference between being either a productive part of your team on the job or just a difficult person to work with.

Communicating

Biotechnologists must relate to people who may have more or less sophisticated education than they do. The knack of communicating on all levels is crucial.

There may be a tendency to view the wonders of biotechnology from an intellectual perspective, forgetting at times the "down-to-earth" duty of keeping customers of your company happy and informed. Biotechnologists, therefore, should possess the sales abilities to tell clients how products will help them.

Regardless if you are a scientist, executive, or marketing person, in a corporate setting you are always selling your ideas. You are attempting to convince others that your thoughts make sense. The more you enjoy and take pride in your work, the more persuasive you will be. If you can get someone to think of something in the same way you do, even if that individual does not come to your same conclusion, you have accomplished a sales job.

Cooperating

In the laboratory, employees must be willing to endure long hours to get a job done and have the perseverance to attack problems from a variety of angles. Work as a team is essential, and information, progress, findings, and other details must be continually shared.

When you are in an actual work situation, do not limit your efforts only to your assigned job. When appropriate, help others in your research group with their projects, and always make sure that you let others know when a change has been made that affects their work, or when you will be using common areas or equipment. This is not to say that you should sacrifice your own work, but it means that you need to think of everyone if you're on a team and do what you can to make others successful, too.

It is essential also to be able to focus upon a goal that has been set by a research and development group. Be dedicated to the completion of the project, but if the priority of the undertaking changes, be able to adjust, to keep in tune with the changing needs.

Making the Most of Experience

Some human resource officers and personnel agencies seek job candidates with B.S. or M.S. degrees who have solid, broad foundations in the hard sciences of chemistry, physics, and mathematics. They believe this background foretells an ability to be versatile on the job. It also indicates learned discipline that will be beneficial to a researcher as he or she moves up the job ladder of biotechnology.

Industry advertising indicates that employers are looking for job candidates with a wide variety of backgrounds and experience. Degrees at all levels in biotechnology are in demand by some employers, and others are looking for traditional backgrounds in biology and chemistry.

If your résumé shows that you have worked in a company that has undergone change, you may be of special worth to some hiring officials. Your job record backs up your ability for being able to adjust to changes and stress, something that might not be so obvious if your work history stated you worked for a very staid or conservative and unchanging employer for a long period of time.

Coping with Frustrations

Those who work in the pharmaceutical end of biotechnology admit to a particular, and currently unavoidable, job frustration. They think they must resign themselves to lengthy waits for new drug approval from the U.S. Food and Drug Administration. Sometimes, this means that interested employees cannot see a project through from inception to completion unless they are willing to pursue such goals over a period of years.

At the same time, research scientists in all areas of biotechnology live with another type of tension—competition. The competitive nature of this demanding field can contribute to job stress.

Of course, it is human nature for a person to want to make a name for her- or himself in a field that is itself making history. Today's reputation is tomorrow's legend. This motivating force to excel is healthy as long as it is exhibited in a positive manner. Competition among firms in the industry should be welcomed, too. The innovation it fosters is good news for all.

The push for progress should proceed on a high moral plane. If you are a scientist reporting what you are doing, you have to communicate the truth. As with all human endeavors, there is always the temptation to enhance the facts, but good scientists record accurately exactly what they see, whether or not it fits into their hopes or their preconceived theories.

The temptation to "fudge" is not unique to biotechnology. Due to the nature of this young and fast-growing science, its practitioners are vulnerable to wanting to make fast strides, but any dishonesty in such a field can be dangerous in many ways—to consumers, to colleagues, and to the individual's career, which would be ruined forever if a fraud was proven. It should be emphasized that intellectual honesty has not been a major problem in biotechnology, and it is not expected to be so in the future by those in the field. But occasionally when a problem occurs, it is always a cause for a major investigation, and it also causes harm to many more people in the industry, not just those who are involved. If anyone needs a reality check, more and more review boards are coming into being to double-check research results in all areas of the field.

Being Sensitive to Public Perceptions

Remember, biotechnologists are altering life-forms. Do not ignore an underlying popular fear that monsters might escape out of some laboratory or that some scientists might deliberately release genetically engineered organisms into the environment. It is smart to stay in touch with public opinion and be able to answer it as it relates to the ethical considerations of biotechnology. Any science that is manipulating nature must be subject to public scrutiny and control, such as legislation and permits.

Polls and surveys have shown that the American people have mixed feelings about biotechnology and its regulation. On the one hand, many believe that the risks of biotechnology have been greatly exaggerated and that unjustified fears of genetic engineering have seriously impeded the development of valuable new drugs and therapies.

Yet while many Americans believe the risks and fears of genetic engineering have been exaggerated, they also express concern about them. Many survey respondents have agreed with statements such as "the potential danger from genetically altered cells and microbes is so great that strict regulations are necessary."

It appears that the public recognizes both the unreasonable fears associated with biotechnology as well as real risks. The former are seen as having delayed significant benefits from this technology. But the public still comes down on the side of strict regulation of the field because it perceives potential dangers from the innovations.

While relatively few members of the general public can articulate any type of specific dangers about what they have heard or read, many believe that genetically engineered products are at least somewhat likely to represent a serious danger to humans or the environment. Such perceived dangers include:

- Creation of antibiotic-resistant diseases
- Production of birth defects in humans
- Creation of herbicide-resistant weeds
- Endangerment of the food supply
- Environmental release of organisms that mutate into a deadly disease
- Change of rainfall patterns
- Increase in rate of plant or animal extinction

Thinking Creatively

Being sympathetic to the real and imagined fears expressed in public opinion polls and having the talent to respond to them are not the only exercises of empathetic thinking you can expect as a future biotechnologist. You will be called upon to visualize many things that, on the surface, laypeople might think to be products of unbridled free thought bordering on science fiction. In reality, they are the results of care and scientific expertise.

Some biotechnologists follow a step-by-step progression and think in an orderly fashion as they move to complete their research projects. Others work best when they experience flashes of insight. It is equally acceptable in this field to methodically heed all the conventional instructions when you work with your laboratory instruments as it is to "play around" with your instruments as you experimentally follow your educated instincts to achieve assigned goals.

Accepting Failure and Starting Again

Regardless of your approach, you must be ready and willing to accept failure. It comes along very often. True, it is hard to take. The joys of success, however, equal or exceed the sorrows of falling short of your expectations. You will not advance in your career if the way you think and act is hindered by an apprehension of failing. Do your best to enjoy your work and its risks, and be ready to learn from your failures and to pick up and start again if a project fails.

Holding on to Interest and Integrity

Sometimes your work may seem to be dragging on a slow, day-to-day basis. Try to spark your excitement with the knowledge that you are heading in the right direction to create something that will be helpful to humanity.

From time to time you may be hearing about or actually confronting desperate individuals pleading for cures and treatments if you are focusing your efforts in disease research. Public or corporate pressure can never be allowed to foster shortcuts, compromise, or haste in the research laboratory. Testing and retesting until the time is right for scientific acceptance should be part of the biotechnologist's creed.

The various aspects of temperament discussed in this chapter can be characterized as the little things that, when blended together, make a biotechnologist candidate more likely to move up the ladder in her or his chosen field.

7

FINDING THE RIGHT JOB

LOOKING FOR THE right job is a familiar activity in our society, and everyone who has experienced "the search" certainly appreciates the value of monster.com and other jobs websites on the Internet, corporate websites, classified newspaper ads, networking with friends and colleagues, and, above all, a hearty supply of perseverance and hope.

Getting Started

As you begin your job search for the best biotechnology job for you, in addition to the Internet, all of the traditional job search strategies and sources are good to know about. These include:

- Classified ads in industry news publications
- Classified ads in international, national, regional, and local news publications
- Conferences, conventions, and job fairs

- Corporations in the field
- Financial organizations
- Government publications
- Networking contacts
- Professional associations
- Professional journals
- Trade and business magazines

In addition, there are some specific strategies that will help you to find a job as a biotechnologist. Some of the techniques described in this chapter are especially applicable to this field, which, as you have seen, is unique in many respects.

Internet Job Search Sites

The Internet is expanding continually in its usefulness as an information source in job searches, and it provides rich resources in many different kinds of websites, both for finding job listings and for learning about potential employers.

Specific biotechnology job services are proliferating on the Internet. Some are general and deal with job and hiring services for any part of bioscience, biotechnology, life sciences and health care, bioagriculture, biochemistry, and others. Some are specific to a single segment of the industry or to a single geographical area. Some are free to job candidates; some charge a fee.

With a simple search for "biotechnology jobs" via Google and Yahoo search engines in 2006, more than 246,000 sites came up, and this number is growing all the time. Many sites provide you with a gold mine of information. In selecting sites to use, you should always check to see whether the site is:

- **Current.** Is the information up-to-date, or is it old?
- **Published by a reputable organization.** Look up any that are unknown.
- **Free or charging only a small fee to job candidates.** High fees are a red flag.
- **Privacy protected.** Always check security before giving any information.

If you do not know whether the website publisher is reliable, do not submit any information. A few established and comprehensive sites are listed below. (This list is intended for information only and does not constitute an endorsement in any way.)

www.hirebio.com

HireBio provides searches for employers, jobs, current discussion topics, and peer networking. Job seekers first must log in and set up an account; then they can post a résumé, search for jobs, receive its newsletter, and use the Salary Wizard, which is continually updated. Biotechnology jobs are categorized by region and specialties, which include: clinical monitoring, project management, clinical research, consulting, medical sales, data management, information technology, and scientific laboratories. The site is published by the Massachusetts Technology Corporation.

www.biospace.com/jobs

BioSpaceJobs is a multifaceted website that offers announcements of upcoming life science career fairs and lists jobs grouped by "hotbed communities." These include: BioCapital (Washington, DC area); BioMidwest (Iowa, Indiana, Illinois, Michigan, Minnesota, Missouri, Ohio, and Wisconsin); BioGarden (New Jersey); BioPenn (Pennsylvania); BioTech Bay (San Francisco); BioTech Beach (Southern California); BioNC (North Carolina); Genetown (Massachusetts); and Pharm Country (Connecticut, New Jersey, New York, Pennsylvania). It provides features on selected employer companies and resources for job search and job planning, including a cost-of-living calculator and job assessor. It is published by Biospace.

www.sciencecareers.org

This American Association for the Advancement of Science website provides job search tools, résumé and cover letter tips, and job alerts, usually for approximately twenty-three hundred jobs. Users must set up an account. It includes a meeting and events feature, an extensive events calendar for the entire year to come, and career development information.

www.biocareer.com

This website is host to the SciWeb Biotechnology Career Center, which provides listings for chemists, pharmaceutical sales, academic postdoctoral (free), and general science jobs. Its features include job search services, résumé posting services, and job posting services, and it is reputedly one of the largest online databases of biotechnology candidates. It is published by SciWeb, Inc.

www.medzilla.com

Medzilla started in 1994 and is one of the best-known job sites on the Web. It provides a search service for job seekers and one for employers. It also has a résumé posting service, résumé editing service, job agent service, forums on selected biotechnology job search topics, and biotechnology articles, and it usually provides information on more than eight thousand jobs. Users must set up an account.

www.clinicalmonitorjobs.com

This site is hosted by Kforce Clinical Research Staffing, as the Kforce Clinical Research Resource Center. It lists clinical research jobs; a recent typical job list included these positions: Regional Clinical Research Associate, In-House Clinical Research Associate, SAS Programmer, Biostatistician, Safety Manager/Associate, Clinical Data Manager, and Medical Research Manager. The site provides a browser with job descriptions and an application form. Jobs are with "biotech and pharmaceutical companies."

Researching Corporations

If you are not already familiar with the corporate work world, it will be helpful for you to gain a general familiarity with various kinds of corporations, their goals, how they work toward these, and how they fail and succeed—in other words, how they do business. Corporate culture and corporate ethics make a great deal of difference in how much you will enjoy a particular job and whether you will want to stay with it. To get a feel for the general business climate in the United States and its most frequent partners, you can regularly browse *Fortune* magazine, *Business Week*, and *U.S. News and World Report*. The *Wall Street Journal* and *New York Times* will also be helpful, with focus that is somewhat more on the financial side. These and other long-established news publications will help you gain an overview of the business world so that you can understand the characteristics that are valued in American and neighboring countries' businesses. With even casual reading in your spare time over a semester, you will begin to recognize many major companies, become familiar with their reputations, and understand how changes in the economic and political environment, in corporate management, in local and global competition, and so forth can change the fortunes of these organizations and, therefore, the fortunes of their employees.

When you are considering a job with a particular corporation, it is important to know as much as possible about that company not only to help you succeed at an interview, but to decide whether you want to apply for a job in the first place. Simply type the company's name into your browser, and see what comes up. For any large corporation, you will probably get at least several items from recent news, from investment analysts' opinions, and from the corporation's own website, which will provide you with an annual report, company history, general description, and much more.

You will want to look for both positives and negatives. Awards, new contracts, fairly steady growth, statements of good principles in the corporate goals, evidence of social and environmental responsibility, and a roster of decent people as officers and on the board of directors will all contribute to make a good impression on you. On the other hand, if the company has a history of double-talking or of avoiding social or environmental responsibility, has board members of questionable character, or has not been open and honest in its dealings with employee pensions or the like, then your faith in the principals of that organization will likely take a nosedive, and you will probably want to avoid it as an employer. Keep in mind that you are looking for the best because you are going to give your best and because you want to be in harmony with the goals of the organization you choose.

You can begin with a company's own website to see what it has to say about itself. Check the website for general information about the company: its mission statement, recent accomplishments, financial health, recent and upcoming events, board of directors and affiliations, employees and officers, and career postings. Check to see if the company is posting any jobs in areas of interest to you. If insider-trading postings are available, check those carefully and note any patterns. Then check a few of the other items that came up on your search, especially news items or analysts' reviews. Briefly check the blogs, too, for any emotional highs or lows being expressed by employees, clients, or customers.

Always keep a file of your notes and important findings for a particular company and the date so you won't have to duplicate your search later. Also save paragraphs or whole items that interest you, and then go on to access another website.

Listed below are examples of some well-known companies in the field of biotechnology, just to get you started. A brief annotation for each company gives you an idea of some of their products and specializations. Choose a few that are working in areas of interest to you, and explore them on the Internet.

- **Amgen.** Therapeutics based on cellular and molecular biology advances
- **Aventis Agriculture.** Animal nutrition, crop science, health, and plant biotechnology
- **Aventis Pharma.** Diagnostics, prescription drugs, therapeutic proteins, and vaccines

- **Biogen, Inc.** Development of human health care drugs using genetic engineering (GE)
- **Chiron Corporation.** Biopharmaceuticals, blood testing, products for cancer and infectious diseases, and vaccines using genomics, recombinant proteins, and small-molecule development methods
- **Corixa.** Research and development to treat and prevent autoimmune diseases, cancer, and infectious diseases by direction of the immune system
- **Genentech, Inc.** Using human genetic information to develop, produce, and market pharmaceuticals that target unmet medical needs
- **Genzyme Corporation.** Divisions are Genzyme Biosurgery, Genzyme General, and Genzyme Molecular Oncology; develops and markets products and services in new areas for unmet medical needs
- **Gilead Sciences.** Medicines for cancer and infectious diseases
- **Hyseq, Inc.** Applies genomics platform in order to develop biopharmaceuticals
- **Immunex Corporation** Biopharmaceutical company dedicated to immune system science innovations
- **Ligand Pharmaceuticals, Inc.** Discovers and develops new drugs that address unmet medical needs in cancer, cardiovascular and inflammatory diseases, hormone-related diseases, metabolic disorders, osteoporosis, and skin diseases
- **Millennium Pharmaceuticals, Inc.** Discovery and development of small-molecule, biotherapeutic (antibodies and proteins), and predictive products; goal is to provide personalized and precisely focused treatment medication by integrating breakthrough therapeutic products and predictive medicines

- **Monsanto.** Products to help crop farmers control unwanted vegetation, increase efficiency of dairy milk production, and provide improved seed for a number of cropping systems
- **Nanogen.** Integrates advanced microelectronics and molecular biology into a platform technology with potential commercial applications in biomedical research, genetic testing, genomics, and medical diagnostics
- **Oxford GlycoSciences.** Integrating proteomics and genomics to build a pipeline of proprietary small molecule and antibody drug and diagnostic products based on portfolio of patent applications relating to disease-associated proteins
- **SkyePharma.** Provides drug delivery services that use inhalable, injectable, nanoparticulate soluble, oral, and topical technologies to major pharmaceutical partners

Learning from the Associations

In the biotechnology industry, you will want to try the websites of the major bioscience and biotechnology associations. Almost every one has a job board, careers, or employment menu to choose from. Click on these and make notes of the ones that interest you. You will soon find that you've got more information than you can manage, so be efficient and choose only the best ones to save to your job-search file.

More than 160 biotechnology-related associations in the United States, Canada, Mexico, Central and South America, Europe, Asia (including China, India, Japan, Korea, and Singapore), Africa, and Australia are listed with their websites in Appendix B. In addition, Appendix C provides a list of a dozen associations focused especially in the field of informatics.

Conferences, Conventions, and Career Fairs

Hundreds of biotechnology conferences are taking place each year in the United States and in many other countries, and the numbers are expanding fast. These are important gathering places for the people in the profession for a number of reasons, including:

- Opportunity to get an overview of your field
- Sharing of ideas and knowledge in intense learning environment
- Dense gathering of professionals with same interests
- Focus on the best and/or cutting-edge ideas, theories, strategies, and technology
- Gathering of exhibitors showing newest and best equipment, publications, supplies, products and services, and/or the accomplishments of their research organizations (remember, every exhibitor is a potential employer)
- Spotlight on leaders in the field and their ideas, excellence, and achievements
- Immediate social introductions to potential employers and also new friends
- Face-to-face communication and awareness of your peers
- Job and career information on bulletin boards, at career and exhibitors' booths, and in daily newsletters
- Possibility of job fairs

To find out about conferences, conventions, and meetings, go to the professional association websites listed in Appendix B and C. Almost all of these organizations advertise annual conferences or conventions and also list other important events in their special part of the field.

It won't take you long to see which are the best conferences for you to attend. Some of the small ones are as important as the big ones, so check out the speakers and the programs to see which ones will best serve your needs and interests. Most of the large organizations and many of the small ones hold conferences at both the national and state levels. In general, smaller meetings and those that are close to home are less expensive than larger ones or those that are far away. If funds are an issue, start with smaller ones that are close to home. You can work your way up, depending on your available time and finances. In addition, you can save costs by checking on student rates for transportation, for membership in the associations, for registration fees for the conferences, and for lodging.

Carefully consider the opportunities presented by all of the gatherings that are held in your own area. Don't miss the excitement and the inspiration that happen at gatherings in your field. Not every meeting is a blockbuster, but there's unequaled excitement in the ones that are. You won't want to miss this unique kind of opportunity to network and to keep up with what's happening in your field.

If your school is an exhibitor and you are asked to work at your school's booth, don't feel as though you're stuck at the table behind the stacks of brochures and papers. It's a terrific opportunity. Get up out of your chair and greet everyone who walks by, whether or not they are stopping to look at your materials. Welcome visitors; offer them literature about your school or a take-away reminder such as a balloon, pencil, or lapel pin with your school's name on it (if you have such an item); and encourage them to sign the guest book or the mailing list. Offer a chair if visitors look tired or as though their feet hurt. Make them feel relaxed and noticed, but don't overdo it. Just be sincere, and they'll be glad to see you again. If they don't stop today, maybe they will tomorrow, and they'll remember you if you're really glad to see them. After a couple of conferences like this, you'll see that people feel as though they know you, and that's good both for your spirit and your job search.

Be sure to get around the exhibit hall, and stop to look at the displays. Absorb as much as possible about the exhibitors, learning more about who are the industry leaders and who is up and coming. Take home literature if you want, but it may be more practical to take home a business card with a website or e-mail address on it. Don't forget that paper is heavy, and you may be carrying all the freebies along with your own luggage on the way home.

When you check out the organizations that have displays, consider them as possible employers. Consider the quality of the display, and talk with people on duty at the table or booth; get a feel for the organization, and get familiar with what each one does. Spend just a little time on each organization until you identify the ones that really interest you; then use the rest of your time to concentrate on those.

Almost all conferences and conventions will have exhibitors. At small ones there may be only four or five exhibits; at the largest ones there are hundreds. At a medium-sized conference in 2006, the thirty-three organizations listed below were exhibitors. Each one of them is an employer, and you'll recognize many of the names.

Accelrys	ISMB 2006
Apple	MCBI
Ariadne Genomics	MIT Press
Biobase Corporation	Ocimum Biosolutions
Biomax Informatics AG	Orion Multisystems
BioMed Central	Oxford University Press
Biosystems Informatics	Partek
Institute	PubGene

The Blueprint Initiative
Cambridge University Press
ECCB 2005–Madrid
Elsevier MDL
EMBL–European
    Bioinformatics Institute
Gene Logic, Inc.
GenomeWeb, LLC
Hewlett-Packard
IBM
ISCB

Public Library of Science
RCSB Protein Data Bank
Springer
Sun Microsystems
Synamatix
TimeLogic
University of Michigan
    Bioinformatics
    Program
Unleashed Informatics,
    Ltd.

Networking

Networking should be a pleasure for you and your contacts. Begin by making up a chart. The first column should list "Names." Write down the professors you most admire, the fellow students you like and respect, and the people in your field whom you have only just met but who have made a good impression on you. Add the school's career counselors and any other good ideas you can think of—people who might know good employers of the kind you want. Allow space for e-mail and mailing addresses and phone numbers, as needed.

Make space on the chart to note "Date of Request" and "Outcomes" for each of these and also a column marked "Thank-you." Then start making your contacts. Enjoy it. Don't take up all of your contacts' time or spend all of your time schmoozing, but enjoy the opportunity to be in touch with these good people, and let them know that you think a lot of their ideas and appreciate their help.

Use e-mail, phone calls, handwritten notes, or formal letters, whichever is most appropriate for each individual request. Ask for information or referrals as appropriate. If you get a negative response, such as there are no jobs available or there is no information the person can give you, this is where *more* networking comes in. Ask if the person can refer you to one or more other persons who might have information or the possibility of a job for you.

Add the new contacts to your list, and note who gave you the name. When the time comes, you'll thank them both.

Another excellent way to make immediate contacts in the entry-level job marketplace is to network with individuals who are the officers, managers, and project leaders responsible for hiring at their research institutes or companies. One way to find these key people is to go to the library and review scientific literature (books, magazines) for names, telephone numbers, and any other appropriate information. Another is to search relevant websites on the Internet, even though your contacts with these individuals will be seemingly just "cold calls" on the telephone or by letter. You should explain concisely who you are and describe your background and current position as a student, intern, or novice in the field. Then you can ask respectfully for information, advice, or an exploratory interview. You may find they will warm up to what you are attempting to do. After all, they were in the same position as you at one time, too. They may give you advice or information or recommend someone to whom you may send a résumé and a letter.

Be sure to keep a record of these requests and their outcomes. Each contact should receive a thank-you letter within the week after his or her response.

Temporary and Contract Work

A good way to get to know a number of companies in a short amount of time is to work for a temporary-worker—or "temp"—

agency. Most of these agencies are in or near large cities, where the number of customer companies makes their business needed. All cities have office temporary agencies, and some areas have temp agencies that supply every imaginable kind of worker, from pharmacists to diamond setters.

People have worked for temp agencies for as little as a week or as long as several years. When you know where you will be spending a vacation period or a summer, you can find out what temp agencies are in the area and what markets they serve. You should apply to the temp agency early and arrange for interviews, skill tests, or other requirements. If you go to work for one of them, you will usually be an employee and not an independent contractor. This means that the temp agency will take out taxes from your paycheck and will make the arrangements with the company where you will work.

Suppose, for example, that the temp agency will send you to be a lab assistant in a pharmaceutical company for a period of three weeks, and you will be working on one particular project for which they need extra help. The temp agency may have contracted with the pharmaceutical company to provide six trained people. All of you will be responsible to get to the pharmaceutical company on your own, on time. You will be given the name of the supervisor there, to whom you will report, and who will sign your timecard at the end of each week. The hourly rates paid to temporary employees are not high, but the advantage to this kind of work is the opportunity to learn a great deal about a company or an institute as an employee—a kind of "taste of the place" approach to job searching. If you work for four or five of these places over a summer, you will possibly have learned more about the industry in that area than many people who have been in it for years.

Another possible advantage is that permanent positions are frequently offered to good temp employees. The temporary agency will have a policy in place about this, so be sure to ask what it is and abide by it. In most cases the potential permanent employer will notify the temp agency that he or she is interested in making a permanent job offer. The temp agency will typically receive a finder's fee for having brought the worker to the potential employer's notice. The worker does not usually have to pay any fee.

Contract or consultant companies operate in a different way. Some of them supply whole workforces in a given project area for long periods of time. This custom has grown in the last fifteen or twenty years, as more companies have decided to outsource big chunks of their work. The contract company may have the contract with the client company, and it actually employs the workers; conversely, each of the workers may make a contract with the client company, which in this case acts like an employment manager. In either of these cases, the contract company usually negotiates top dollar for its own services and for the salary or wage that is paid to the workers. If the worker contracts individually with the client company, that worker is legally an independent contractor, which means that he or she must send in his or her own income taxes, keep his or her own books, and do all of the other chores of being a sole proprietor business.

This kind of work arrangement has some of the advantages of being a temp in that you can check out a company without actually investing yourself in becoming an employee. It usually pays well and is sometimes more readily available in tight job markets. One reason for this is that it saves the client company money because the company can have a larger workforce for a temporary need without having to hire the workers. Also, the company does not usually pay for medical insurance or other benefits.

Experiencing the work of the client company is limited to the special project or area of the contract, but it is a professional experience nonetheless. The contract worker carries concrete responsibility for project development and corporate products and services, often with a surprising degree of autonomy. The most serious drawback is that contract companies often have difficulty supervising their various groups of workers, even if there is provision for their supervisors to be on-site at the client premises. It is hard to maintain orderly and practical supervision in situations where many workers are serving two masters, and communication is complicated and sometimes at cross-purposes.

If you decide to accept a temporary contract work situation, be ready to work without many traditional policies and procedures being in place. Be prepared to make extra efforts to communicate and to be patient while policies are instituted and procedures are invented on the spot. If possible, get information and advice from friends and colleagues who have already done the job. Especially in a scientific setting, where coordination and precision are essential, it can feel a lot like heading for the North Pole behind a sled pulled by basset hounds and alley cats.

The best side effect of being one of the workers in an outsourced project is that you can make a lot of informative contacts. Contract workers in the United States are often beginners in the field, mid-life career changers, or laid-off workers, all of whom are considering what they are going to do next. As professionals in transition, all these people have experiences to share and usually an eagerness to learn from each other. Before you finish the project and go your separate ways, collect e-mail addresses and phone numbers and add the best ones to your contact list.

Cover Letters and Résumés

Having researched potential employers and networked with contacts in the field, you are ready to pursue a permanent job. The next step is to prepare your cover letter and résumé and send them to the key contacts you have made.

Cover Letter

The cover letter is an introductory narrative that gives its reader a taste of the applicant's qualifications and appropriateness for the job. The letter should mention what career directions you want to take, why you would be a plus in a biotechnology organization, and a little about where you want to go with your life in this industry. The cover letter should not be long; that kind of detail is what your résumé is for. Make the cover letter two or three paragraphs at most, and be sure it is carefully written. It's also a good idea to have someone else proofread it for typographical and grammatical errors.

Résumé

It is helpful to have more than one résumé if you have different interests you would like to pursue. An entry-level person should concentrate on style, form, and how well the résumé is written.

To avoid the somewhat wooden tone of some professionally written résumés that have been created in a résumé shop, it is better for you to develop your résumé yourself, even if you have little experience. If you truly have no work experience to cite, it may help to focus upon your academic skills and professional goals rather than on what you have done in the past.

Make sure the information you include on your résumé is relevant. Leave out personal information about family, hobbies, and religious, recreational, and community activities. Companies are interested in seeing information about your potential commercial value to them and will appreciate succinct information about your education, special skills, and any research experience you have.

There is an advantage in preparing your résumé on a computer and changing the arrangement of the text in different ways to fit the operational requirements of different companies. You may, for instance, have an interest in large-scale mammalian cell culture and working for a production house that manufactures pharmaceuticals. On the other hand, you may consider it rewarding to sell the instrumentation that does this process. Two different résumés might emphasize the two different things so that your interest and experience for each specific kind of job will show up to best advantage. Your overall job statement on each résumé should be specific and to the point and should relate to the job you are applying for.

Résumés for e-mailing or posting on the Internet must be written differently from those that are printed on paper. Electronic messages should be much more succinct, with shorter sentences and more white space. The electronic form should still present your information in one column, but the lines of text should be no more than sixty-two characters wide. For best ease of reading and for emphasis, you may want to use a serif font such as Times New Roman for the body of the text in your print résumés and a sans-serif font such as Arial for use in the shorter form you will use on the Internet.

Follow-Up Phone Calls

Making follow-up telephone calls to each of your contacts is the next step. You will find that about 60 to 70 percent of them will make themselves available to you after they receive your letter.

One good way to give yourself credibility when you are at entry level without any professional experience is to reference your professors. If there is ongoing communication between some of your professors and the companies or research institutes you are contacting, mention the name of your thesis advisor or point out that you served as research assistant to a particular professor, for example. Some companies ask professors to report the names of top graduating students to them, and if you have this kind of entree, you will, of course, discuss the work that you have done with those professors.

Be realistic about the level of job you are qualified for, and show a dynamic interest and enthusiasm about what the company does. Make your letter direct, friendly, businesslike, and respectful. You do not want your letter to look like a form letter that is being sent off to many different companies. Hiring officials can quickly spot a letter that appears to have been mass produced by a résumé service. That is why it is important that you mention specific things not only about your skills and goals, but also about the company in which you are interested.

Succeeding at Interviews

The interview process can be a stressful one, but it needn't be. Here is some advice to help you smooth the way.

Phone Interviews

Some biotechnology companies do their initial interviewing over the telephone, so you will need to sharpen your telephone skills. This includes predetermining the time when someone is going to call. Make certain you have notes that will help you with your role in the conversation. Ask intelligent questions, since you do not have a great deal of experience to talk about. Mention your career goals. Check the company website and literature, the trade press, and the business press to find information about the company's products, its customers, its rank in the industry, and its current plans. Have all this "spontaneous" conversation pretty well rehearsed so it flows well on the telephone.

The company spokesperson to whom you will be talking first may be a scientist who needs a technician and who thought your cover letter looked interesting. You might be surprised at how many mature scientists feel somewhat uncomfortable in telephone interviews, so there is no reason why your conversation should not be two-sided in terms of the questions being asked. Be as congenial as possible within the limits of good business conversation.

Send out as many letters as possible to a variety of companies. Recruiters say that, traditionally, it used to take an average of ten letters to get an interview, and ten interviews to get an offer, but in tight job markets, the average is a lot more.

Personal Interviews

Scientists do have the authority to hire people. Sometimes job applicants will get a second telephone call from the company's human resources representative, who may be putting together the details for a personal appearance at the home office. If you have to travel for this interview, the trip is usually at the firm's expense, and it will usually arrange the tickets and hotel reservations, as well. You need to confirm this, and it's acceptable to ask immediately, when the company representative asks if you will be available to make the trip.

The entry-level interview is typical of those in other industries. If you are a job candidate with a bachelor's degree and have no previous experience working in the biotechnology field, you can expect to spend some time at the human resources department filling out forms. You will get a complete orientation regarding the past, present, and future of your host company. You will probably tour the facilities and meet some of the people in the firm's groups.

Many companies in biotechnology have a laid-back, short-sleeved attitude. Quite a few of the employees you will see are casual in their appearance. Do not let that informality fool you, however. Your clothing and hair are still important. Factors like grooming, poise, and posture are an important part of your self-presentation and will be weighed along with your intellectual promise.

Above all, keep in mind that biotechnology firms are entrepreneurial enterprises. You will have to convince hiring officials that you are serious both about your future and that of their company. The founders of these firms have worked long hours. Do not be surprised if you are called upon to do the same.

It is crucial that you emphasize how you are going to benefit the company. Emphasize your goals that coincide with those of the firm and, even more specifically, with those of the work area of the person who is interviewing you.

Watch how you sit in your chair. Note the body language of the interviewer. If he or she is leaning forward, you might lean forward, too. However, do not get so preoccupied with picking up on the interviewer's mannerisms that you lose track of what is being said.

The tips that follow can help add to a successful interview.

- Smile when it's natural to do so.
- Be courteous to everyone you meet at the company.
- Try to maintain eye contact with your interviewer.
- Be relaxed, but maintain good posture.

- Do not sit rigidly still. You can gesture and move a bit when appropriate.
- Always be accurate and tell the truth.

As an entry-level job candidate, you should control the conversation about 40 percent of the time. It's good when you show enough interest in your future employer to ask questions about his or her company's history and its future potential. These queries should be planned and reviewed in advance. Many hiring officials decide upon the worth of job applicants by the quality of the questions they ask.

Once you have completed your job interview, you will have to wait while company officials consider your chances for employment. You can usually anticipate a quick decision.

Working with Recruiters

It is common to change from one aspect of biotechnology into some other area of specialization. There is a great deal of horizontal movement in the areas of operations, manufacturing, quality control, and regulatory affairs. People move back and forth between all of these disciplines.

When a person already is in the biotechnology business and is planning a career move within the industry, recruiters can be most helpful. There is great variety in "head hunters" out there. They fill job assignments that companies give them, which accounts for 80 percent of their activities.

If you bring yourself to the attention of a recruiter who is impressed with you, he or she will go to bat for you, making contacts on your behalf with the objective of making a placement.

A good recruiter screens his or her clients. The thing that is important to a recruiter is the client's seriousness in making a move. The recruiter will want to establish why an individual wants to leave one job for another.

Recruiters are not employment agencies and they do not charge fees to the job candidates. Companies pay that expense because they need to find good people.

If someone wants to make a move within the biotechnology industry without the aid of a recruiter, there is always the danger of jeopardizing confidentiality somewhere down the road. There is a chance that one's present employer will learn of the job search. Recruiters, on the other hand, will call as many companies as it takes without releasing an individual's name.

The best way to contact a recruiter is by word of mouth from trusted colleagues, by checking on the Internet, and by reading trade magazines, industry listings, and material put out by trade associations. You can scan membership lists of these organizations, when available, for member recruiters.

Choosing Well in an Expanding Field

Everyone has opinions regarding whether it is better to work for a small company or a large one, a start-up or a well-established organization. Your own personality and preferences will determine what is right for you.

You may prefer being surrounded by the trappings of a large company that offers solid traditions and procedures and outstanding benefits. Or, you might prefer to wear all types of hats and be able to experience rapid career growth, in which case you will be more likely to find this combination of opportunities at a small company, and there are even more of those in this fast-growing field.

One of the exciting things about a career in biotechnology is that you can choose from a great many growing and still-expanding career options in almost every part of the field. Biotechnology provides well-prepared young people with a ground-floor opportunity today in a field that is so dynamic that its many varied options are only increasing.

Appendix A

Biotechnology Time Line

This time line of major occurrences in the development of biotechnology has been excerpted from material supplied by the Biotechnology Industry Organization.

8000 b.c.

- Humans domesticate crops and livestock.
- Potatoes are cultivated for food.

4000–2000 b.c.

- Biotechnology is used to leaven bread and ferment beer using yeast (Egypt).
- Production of cheese and fermentation of wine (Sumeria, China, and Egypt) occurs.
- Babylonians control date palm breeding by pollinating female trees with pollen from certain male trees.

500 b.c.

- First known antibiotic is used: moldy soybean curds are used to treat boils (China).

A.D. 100

- First known insecticide discovered: powdered chrysanthemums (China).

1322

- An Arab chieftain uses artificial insemination to produce superior horses.

1590

- Janssen invents the microscope.

1663

- Hooke discovers the existence of the cell.

1675

- Leeuwenhoek discovers bacteria.

1761

- Koelreuter reports successful crossbreeding of crop plants in different species.

1797

- Jenner inoculates a child with a viral vaccine to protect him from getting smallpox.

1830–1833

- Proteins are discovered (1830).
- First enzyme is discovered and isolated (1833).

1835–1855

- Schleiden and Schwann propose that all organisms are composed of cells, and Virchow declares, "Every cell arises from a cell."

1857

- Pasteur proposes microbes cause fermentation.

1859

- Darwin publishes the theory of evolution by natural selection. The concept of carefully selecting parents and culling variable progeny greatly influences plant and animal breeders in the late 1800s, despite ignorance of the scientific basis of genetics.

1865

- The science of genetics begins: Austrian monk Gregor Mendel studies garden peas and discovers that genetic traits are passed from parents to offspring in a predictable way: the laws of heredity.

1870–1890

- Using Darwin's theory, plant breeders crossbreed cotton, developing hundreds of varieties with superior qualities.
- Farmers inoculate fields with nitrogen-fixing bacteria in order to improve yields.
- Beal produces first experimental corn hybrid in the laboratory.
- Koch develops a technique for staining and identifying bacteria (1877).
- Laval develops the first centrifuge (1878).
- Fleming discovers chromatin, the rodlike structures in the cell nucleus that later came to be called chromosomes (1879).

1900

- Drosophila (fruit flies) are used in early studies of genes.

1902

- The term *immunology* first appears.

1906

- The term *genetics* is introduced.

1911

- Rous discovers the first cancer-causing virus.

1914

- Bacteria are used to treat sewage in Manchester, England.

1915

- Phages, or bacterial viruses, are discovered.

1919

- First use of word *biotechnology* occurs in print.

1920

- Evans and Long discover the human growth hormone.

1928

- Fleming discovers penicillin as an antibiotic.
- Small-scale test of formulated *Bacillus thuringiensis* (Bt) for corn borer control begins in Europe. Commercial production of this biopesticide begins in France in 1938.
- Karpechenko crosses radishes and cabbages, creating fertile offspring between plants in different genera.
- Laibach first uses embryo rescue to obtain hybrids from wide crosses in crop plants—known today as *hybridization.*

1930

- U.S. Congress passes the Plant Patent Act, enabling the products of plant breeding to be patented.

1933

- Hybrid corn, developed by Wallace in the 1920s, is commercialized. Growing hybrid corn eliminates the option of saving seeds. The remarkable yields outweigh the increased costs of annual seed purchases, and by 1945 hybrid corn accounts for 78 percent of U.S.-grown corn.

1938

- The term *molecular biology* is coined.

1941

- The term *genetic engineering* is first used by Danish microbiologist A. Jost in a lecture on reproduction in yeast at the technical institute in Lwow, Poland.

1942

- The electron microscope is used to identify and characterize a bacteriophage, a virus that infects bacteria.
- Penicillin is mass-produced in microbes.

1944

- DNA is proven to carry genetic information (Avery et al.).
- Waksman isolates streptomycin, an effective antibiotic for tuberculosis.

1946

- It is discovered that genetic material from different viruses can be combined to form a new type of virus, an example of genetic recombination.

- Recognizing the threat posed by loss of genetic diversity, the U.S. Congress provides funds for systematic and extensive plant collection, preservation, and introduction.

1947

- McClintock discovers transposable elements, or "jumping genes," in corn.

1949

- Pauling shows that sickle cell anemia is a "molecular disease" resulting from a mutation in the protein molecule hemoglobin.

1951

- Artificial insemination of livestock using frozen semen is accomplished.

1953

- The scientific journal *Nature* publishes Watson and Crick's manuscript describing double helical structure of DNA, marking the beginning of the modern era of genetics.

1955

- An enzyme involved in synthesis of a nucleic acid is isolated for the first time.

1956

- Kornberg discovers enzyme DNA polymerase I, leading to understanding of how DNA is replicated.

1958

- Sickle cell anemia is shown to occur due to a change of a single amino acid.
- DNA is made in test tube for first time.

1950s

- Discovery of interferons is made.
- First synthetic antibiotic is developed.
- Systemic fungicides are developed. The steps in protein biosynthesis are delineated (1959).

1960

- Exploiting base pairing, hybrid DNA-RNA molecules are created. Messenger RNA is discovered.

1961

• USDA registers first biopesticide: *Bacillus thuringiensis*, or Bt.

1963

• Wheat varieties developed by Borlaug increase yields by 70 percent.

1964

• The International Rice Research Institute in the Philippines starts the Green Revolution with new strains of rice that double the yield of previous strains if given sufficient fertilizer.

1965

• Harris and Watkins successfully fuse mouse and human cells.

1966

• The genetic code is cracked, demonstrating that a sequence of three nucleotide bases (a *codon*) determines each of twenty amino acids (two more discovered since).

1967

• Automatic protein sequencer is perfected.

1969

• An enzyme is first synthesized in vitro.

1970

• Borlaug receives the Nobel Peace Prize (see 1963).
• The discovery of restriction enzymes that cut and splice genetic material, opening the way for gene cloning, is made.

1971

• First complete synthesis of a gene occurs.

1972

• The DNA composition of humans is discovered to be 99 percent similar to that of chimpanzees and gorillas.
• Initial work with embryo transfer is performed.

1973

• Cohen and Boyer perfect techniques to cut and paste DNA (using restriction enzymes and ligases) and reproduce the new DNA in bacteria.

1974

- The National Institutes of Health (NIH) forms a Recombinant DNA Advisory Committee to oversee recombinant genetic research.

1975

- Government is first urged to develop guidelines for regulating experiments in recombinant DNA: Asilomar Conference, California.
- The first monoclonal antibodies are produced.

1976

- Tools of recombinant DNA are first applied to a human inherited disorder.
- Molecular hybridization is used for prenatal diagnosis of alpha thalassemia.
- Yeast genes are expressed in *E. coli* bacteria.
- Sequence of DNA base pairs for a specific gene are determined.
- First guidelines for recombinant DNA experiments are released (National Institutes of Health Recombinant DNA Advisory Committee).

1977

- First expression of human gene in bacteria occurs.
- Procedures are developed for rapidly sequencing long sections of DNA using electrophoresis.

1978

- High-level structure of virus is first identified.
- Recombinant human insulin is first produced.
- North Carolina scientists show it is possible to introduce specific mutations at specific sites in a DNA molecule.

1979

- Human growth hormone is first synthesized.

Also in the 1970s

- First commercial company is founded to develop genetically engineered products.
- Polymerases are discovered.
- Techniques for rapid sequencing of nucleotides are worked on and perfected.
- Gene targeting occurs.
- RNA splicing occurs.

1980

- U.S. Supreme Court, in landmark case *Diamond* v. *Chakrabarty*, approves the principle of patenting organisms, which allows the Exxon oil company to patent an oil-eating microorganism.
- U.S. patent for gene cloning is awarded to Cohen and Boyer.
- First gene-synthesizing machine is developed.
- Researchers introduce a human gene—one that codes for the protein interferon—into a bacterium.
- Nobel Prize in chemistry is awarded for the creation of the first recombinant molecule: Berg, Gilbert, and Sanger.

1981

- Scientists at Ohio University produce the first transgenic animals by transferring genes from other animals into mice.
- A Chinese scientist becomes the first to clone a fish: a golden carp.

1982

- Applied Biosystems, Inc., introduces first commercial gas phase protein sequencer, dramatically reducing the amount of protein sample needed for sequencing.
- First recombinant DNA vaccine for livestock is developed.
- First biotech drug is approved by FDA: human insulin is produced in genetically modified bacteria.
- First genetic transformation of a plant cell occurs: petunia.

1983

- The polymerase chain reaction (PCR) technique is conceived. PCR, which uses heat and enzymes to make unlimited copies of genes and gene fragments, later becomes a major tool in biotechnology research and product development worldwide.
- First genetic transformation of plant cells by TI plasmids is performed.
- First artificial chromosome is synthesized.
- First genetic markers for specific inherited diseases are found.
- First whole plant is grown from biotechnology: petunia.
- First proof that modified plants pass their new traits to offspring occurs: petunia.

1984

- The DNA fingerprinting technique is developed.
- The entire genome of the human immunodeficiency virus (HIV) is cloned and sequenced.

1985

- Genetic markers for kidney disease and cystic fibrosis are found.
- Genetic fingerprinting is entered as evidence in a courtroom.
- Transgenic plants resistant to insects, viruses, and bacteria are first field-tested.
- NIH approves guidelines for performing gene-therapy experiments in humans.

1986

- First recombinant vaccine for humans is developed: hepatitis B.
- First anticancer drug is produced through biotech: interferon.
- The U.S. government publishes the *Coordinated Framework for Regulation of Biotechnology,* establishing more stringent regulations for rDNA organisms than for those produced with traditional genetic modification techniques.
- A University of California–Berkeley chemist describes how to combine antibodies and enzymes (abzymes) to create pharmaceuticals.
- First field tests of transgenic plants (tobacco) are conducted.
- The Environmental Protection Agency approves release of first transgenic crop: gene-altered tobacco plants.
- The Organization of Economic Cooperation and Development (OECD) Group of National Experts on Safety in Biotechnology states: "Genetic changes from rDNA techniques will often have inherently greater predictability compared to traditional techniques" and "risks associated with rDNA organisms may be assessed in generally the same way as those associated with non-rDNA organisms."

1987

- First approval for field test of modified food plants is given: virus-resistant tomatoes.
- Frostban, a genetically altered bacterium that inhibits frost formation on crop plants, is field-tested on strawberry and potato plants in California, the first authorized outdoor tests of a recombinant bacterium.

1988

- Harvard molecular geneticists are awarded first U.S. patent for genetically altered animal—a transgenic mouse.
- Patent for process to make bleach-resistant protease enzymes to use in detergents is awarded.
- Congress funds Human Genome Project, a massive effort to map and sequence the human genetic code as well as the genomes of other species.

1989

- First approval is given for field test of modified cotton: insect-protected (Bt) cotton.
- Plant Genome Project begins.

Also in the 1980s

- Studies of DNA are used to determine evolutionary history.
- Recombinant DNA animal vaccine is approved for use in Europe.
- Microbes are used in oil spill cleanup: bioremediation technology.
- Ribozymes and retinoblastomas are identified.

1990

- Chy-Max, an artificially produced form of the chymosin enzyme for cheese-making, is introduced. It is the first product of recombinant DNA technology in the U.S. food supply.
- The Human Genome Project—an international effort to map all genes in the human body—is launched.
- First experimental gene therapy treatment is performed successfully on a four-year-old girl suffering from an immune disorder.
- First transgenic dairy cow—used to produce human milk proteins for infant formula—is created.
- First insect-protected corn is developed: Bt corn.
- First food product of biotechnology is approved in the U.K.: modified yeast.
- First field test of a genetically modified vertebrate occurs: trout.

1992

- American and British scientists unveil a technique for testing embryos in vitro for genetic abnormalities such as cystic fibrosis and hemophilia.
- The FDA declares that transgenic foods are "not inherently dangerous" and do not require special regulation.

1993

- Merger of two trade associations creates Biotechnology Industry Organization.
- FDA approves bovine somatotropin (BST) for increased milk production.

1994

- First FDA approval is given for a whole food produced through biotechnology: FLAVRSAVR tomato.
- First breast cancer gene is discovered.

- Recombinant version of human DNase, which breaks down protein accumulation in lungs of cystic fibrosis patients, is approved.
- BST is commercialized as POSILAC bovine somatotropin.

1995

- First baboon-to-human bone marrow transplant is performed on AIDS patient.
- First full gene sequence of a living organism other than a virus is completed, for the bacterium *Hemophilus influenzae.*
- Immune system modulation, gene therapy, and recombinantly produced antibodies enter war against cancer.

1996

- Discovery of gene associated with Parkinson's disease provides new avenue of research into cause and potential treatment of the neurological ailment.

1997

- First animal is cloned from an adult cell in Scotland: a sheep named Dolly.
- First weed- and insect-resistant biotech crops are commercialized: Roundup Ready soybeans and Bollgard insect-protected cotton.
- Biotech crops are grown commercially on nearly five million acres worldwide: Argentina, Australia, Canada, China, Mexico, and the United States.
- Oregon researcher group claims to have cloned two Rhesus monkeys.

1998

- University of Hawaii scientists clone three generations of mice from nuclei of adult ovarian cumulus cells.
- Human embryonic stem cell lines are established.
- Scientists at Japan's Kinki University clone eight identical calves using cells taken from a single adult cow.
- First complete animal genome, for *C. elegans* worm, is sequenced.
- Rough draft of human genome map is produced, showing locations of more than thirty thousand genes.
- Five Southeast Asian countries form consortium to develop disease-resistant papayas.

Also in the 1990s

- First conviction using genetic fingerprinting in the United Kingdom is made.
- Discovery that hereditary colon cancer is caused by defective DNA repair gene is made.

- Recombinant rabies vaccine is tested in raccoons.
- Biotechnology-based biopesticide is approved for sale in United States.
- Patents are issued for mice with specific transplanted genes.
- First European patent on a transgenic animal is issued for transgenic mouse sensitive to carcinogens.

2000

- First complete map of a plant genome is developed: *Arabidopsis thaliana*.
- Biotech crops are grown on 108.9 million acres in thirteen countries.
- "Golden rice" announcement allows the technology to be available to developing countries in hopes of improving health of undernourished people and preventing some forms of blindness.
- First biotech crop is field-tested in Kenya: virus-resistant sweet potato.
- Rough draft of human genome sequence is announced.

2001

- First complete map of the genome of a food plant is completed: rice.
- Chinese National Hybrid researchers report developing a "super rice" that could produce double the yield of normal rice.
- Complete DNA sequencing of the agriculturally important bacteria *Sinorhizobium meliloti*, a nitrogen-fixing species, and *Agrobacterium tumefaciens*, a plant pest, is done.
- A single gene from *Arabidopsis* is inserted into tomato plants to create first crop able to grow in salty water and soil.

2002

- First draft of functional map of yeast proteome, entire network of protein complexes and interactions, is completed (yeast genome map published 1996).
- International consortia sequence genomes of parasite that causes malaria and species of mosquito that transmits the parasite.
- Draft version of complete map of the human genome is published, and first part of the Human Genome Project comes to an end ahead of schedule.
- Scientists make great progress in elucidating factors that control differentiation of stem cells, identifying more than two hundred genes involved in the process.
- Biotech crops are grown on 145 million acres in sixteen countries, a 12 percent increase in acreage grown in 2001. More than one-quarter (27 percent) of global acreage was grown in nine developing countries.
- Researchers announce successful results for vaccine against cervical cancer, the first demonstration of a preventative vaccine for a type of cancer.

- Scientists complete draft sequence of most important pathogen of rice, a fungus that destroys enough rice to feed sixty million people annually. By combining understanding of genomes of fungus and rice, scientists will elucidate molecular basis of interactions between the plant and pathogen.
- Scientists forced to rethink view of RNA when they discover how important small pieces of RNA are in controlling many cell functions.

2003

- Researchers find vulnerability gene for depression and make strides in detecting genetic links to schizophrenia and bipolar disorder.
- GloFish, the first biotech pet, hits North American market. Bred to detect water pollutants, it glows red under black light, thanks to addition of natural fluorescence gene.
- Worldwide biotech crop acreage rises 15 percent to 167.2 million acres in eighteen countries. Brazil and the Philippines grow biotech crops for the first time in 2003. Indonesia allows consumption of imported biotech foods; China and Uganda accept biotech crop imports.
- The U.K. approves first commercial biotech crop in eight years, a biotech herbicide-resistant corn used for cattle feed.
- The U.S. Environmental Protection Agency approves first transgenic root worm-resistant corn, which may save farmers $1 billion annually in crop losses and pesticide use.
- An endangered species—the banteng—is cloned for the first time; 2003 brought other cloning firsts, including mules, horses, and deer.
- Dolly, the cloned sheep that made headlines in 1997, is euthanized after developing progressive lung disease. Dolly was the first successful clone of a mammal.
- Japanese researchers develop biotech naturally decaffeinated coffee bean.

2004

- The FDA approves first anti-angiogenic drug for cancer: Avastin (bevacizumab).
- The FDA clears first DNA microarray test system, the AmpliChip Cytochrome P450 Genotyping Test, to aid in selecting medications and disease for wide variety of common conditions.
- An RNA-interference product for age-related "wet" macular degeneration becomes first RNA product to enter a clinical trial.
- The United Nations Food and Agriculture Organization (FAO) endorses biotech crops and states biotechnology is a complementary tool to traditional farming methods that can help poor farmers and consumers in developing nations.

- The National Academy of Sciences' Institute of Medicine (IOM) finds biotech crops do not pose more health risks than crops created by other techniques, and that food safety evaluations should be based on resulting food product, not technique used to create it.
- FDA finds biotech wheat safe after a food safety review.
- Monsanto introduces low-linolenic soybeans (produced through conventional breeding methods) that will reduce or eliminate trans fatty acids in processed soybean oil.
- Chicken genome is sequenced by the Chicken Genome Sequencing Consortium.
- First cloned pet, a kitten, is delivered to its owner.

BIO Sources: *Access Excellence; Biotech 90: Into the Next Decade,* G. Steven Burrill with Ernst & Young High Technology Group; Biotechnology Industry Organization; Genentech, Inc.; *Genetic Engineering News;* International Food Information Council; International Service for the Acquisition of Agri-Biotech Applications; *ISB News Report; Science; Science News; The Scientist;* Texas Society for Biomedical Research.

Appendix B

Biotechnology-Related Associations and Organizations

AAAS (American Association for the Advancement of Science), www.aaas.org

ABO (Ausbiotech Ltd), www.ausbiotech.org

ADEBIO (French Association on Biotechnology and Bioindustry), www.adebio.org

AfricaBio, www.africabio.com

Agricultural Biotechnology Support Project, www.iia.msu.edu/absp

Agriculture and Environment Biotechnology Commission (United Kingdom), www.aebc.gov.uk

AgroBIO Mexico, www.agrobiomexico.org

Ag-West Biotech, Inc. (Canada), www.agwest.sk.ca

Alaska Fisheries Development Foundation, www.afdf.org

All India Biotech Association (AIBA), www.aibaonline.com

American Academy of Health Physics, www.hps1.org/aahp

American Association of Physicists in Medicine,
    www.aapm.org
American Australian Association,
    www.americanaustralian.org
APBIO (Associação Portuguesa de Bioindústrias)
    (Portugal), www.apbio.pt
Arizona BioIndustry Association, www.azbioindustry.org
Arkansas Biotechnology Association,
    http://biology.uark.edu/aba
Asociación Espanola de Bioempresas (ASEBIO) (Spain),
    www.asebio.com
Assobiotec, The Italian Industrial Association for the
    Development of Bioindustry, www.assobiotec.it
Association of Biomolecular Resource Facilities (ABF),
    www.abrf.org
Association of German Biotechnology Companies (VBU),
    www.v-b-u.org
AusBiotech (Australian Biotechnology Association),
    www.ausbiotech.org
Australian Society for Biophysics, www.biophysics.org.au
Austrian Society for Biotechnology, www.boku.ac.at/ocgbt
Bay Area Bioscience Center, www.baybio.org
BC Biotech (Canada), www.bcbiotech.ca
Belgian Bioindustries Association (BBA), www.bba-bio.be
Belgian Biophysical Society,
    www.chemkuleuven.ac.be/research/bio
BelgoBiotech Educational Website (Belgium),
    www.belgobiotech.be
Beowulf Genomics (United Kingdom),
    www.wellcome.ac.uk

BIA Scotland, www.bioindustry.org

BIO (Biotechnology Industry Organization), www.bio.org

BIO Northern Ireland Bioengineering Center, www.nibec.ulst.ac.uk

Bio Update (Netherlands and United Kingdom), www.bioupdate.com

BioAlberta (Canada), www.bioalberta.com

BIOAtlantech, www.bioatlantech.nb.ca

Biochemical Society (United Kingdom), www.biochemsoc.org.uk

BIOCOM SanDiego, www.biocom.org

Bio-East (Canada), www.bioeast.ca

BioFlorida, www.bioflorida.com

BioIndustry Association (United Kingdom), www.bioindustry.org

Biomedical Biotechnology Center (BBC) (United Kingdom), www.uamsbiotech.com

BioNova, The Nova Scotia Biotechnology and Life Sciences Industry Association, www.bionova.ns.ca

Biophysical Society, www.biophysics.org

Biophysical Society of Canada, www.uqtr.ca

Biophysical Society of Japan, www.biophys.jp

BIOQuébec, www.bioquebec.com

BIOTECanada, www.biotech.ca

Biotech Medical Management Association, www.bmma.org

Biotech Scotland, www.locate-dundee.co.uk

Biotechnology Association of Alabama, www.bioalabama.com

Biotechnology Association of Maine (BAM),
www.mainebiotech.org

Biotechnology Australia, www.biotechnology.gov.au

Biotechnology Council of New Jersey, www.biotechnj.org

Biotechnology Information Institute, www.bioinfo.com

Biotechnology Programme–Euro,
http://ec.europa.eu/research/bio1.html

Biotechnology at the University of California–Berkeley,
www.ucbiotech.org

British Biophysical Society, www.cryst.bbk.ac.uk/BBS

British Columbia Biotechnology Alliance (BCBA),
www.bcbiotech.ca

California Healthcare Institute (CHI), www.chi.org

California Separation Science Society (CaSSS),
www.casss.org

Canadian Biotechnology Advisory Committee, www.cbac-cccb.ca

Canadian Institute of Biotechnology, www.biotech.ca

Center for Advanced Biotechnology and Medicine, Rutgers
University, www.cabm.umdnj.edu

Center for Advanced Research in Biotechnology,
University of Maryland, www.carb.umbi.umd.edu

Center for Biomedical Imaging Technology, University of
Connecticut, www.bme.uconn.edu

Center of Marine Biotechnology, University of Maryland,
www.umbi.umd.edu

Colorado Biotechnology Association,
www.cobioscience.com

Connecticut's Bioscience Cluster (CURE–Connecticut
United for Research Excellence, Inc.), www.curenet.org

DECHEMA, Gesellschaft für Chemische Technik und
  Biotechnologie e.V (Germany), www.dechema.de
Delaware Biotechnology Institute, www.dbi.udel.edu
Deutsche Industrievereinigung Biotechnologie (DIB)
  (German Association of Biotechnology Industries),
  www.vci.de/dib
Development Center for Biotechnology (Taiwan),
  www.dcb.org.tw
Edison Biotechnology Center (Omeris),
  www.ohiou.edu/biotech
The Electrophoresis Society, www.aesociety.org
EuropaBIO, www.europabio.org
European Biophysical Societies' Association, www.ebsa.org
European Federation of Biotechnology, www.efbweb.org
Finnish Bioindustries, www.finbio.net
Food and Agriculture Organization of the United Nations,
  www.fao.org
Food Biotechnology Communications Network, University
  of Guelph, Canada, www.foodsafetynetwork.ca/en
Foro Argentino de Biotecnología (FAB), www.foarbi.org.ar
France Biotech, www.france-biotech.org
Fundação BIOMINAS (Brazil), www.biominas.org.br
Georgia Biomedical Partnership,
  www.gabio.org/overview.asp
Harvard Gene Therapy Initiative, Harvard University,
  www.hgti.med.harvard.edu
Hawaii Biotechnology Council (HBC),
  www.hawaii.gov/dbedtert/archive/biotec
Hong Kong Institute of Biotechnology (HKIB),
  www.hkib.org.hk

Illinois Biotechnology Industry Organization (IBIO),
www.ibio.org

Indian National Science Academy, www.insa.ac.in

Indiana Health Industry Forum, www.ihif.org

Institute of Biochemistry and Biophysics (IBB) (Poland),
www.kpk.gov.pl/prog_hor_1/Embeu.htm

Institute for Biotechnology Information,
www.bioinfo.com

Institute for Human Gene Therapy, University of
Pennsylvania, www.upenn.edu

Institute of Molecular Biotechnology (IMB) (Germany),
www.imb-jena.de

International Centre for Genetic Engineering and
Biotechnology (ICGEB) (New Delhi, India, and
Trieste, Italy), www.icgeb.org

International Forum for Genetic Engineering and the
Intrinsic Value and Integrity of Animals and Plants
(Edinburgh), www.ifgene.org

International Institute of Biophysics, Coherence in Biology,
Biocommunication, Biophotonics (Germany, fourteen
Institutes), www.lifescientists.de

International Organization for Medical Physics (sixteen
thousand medical physicists worldwide and seventy-four
member organizations), www.iomp.org

International Union for Pure and Applied Biophysics,
www.iupab.org

Iowa Biotechnology Association, www.iowabiotech.com

Irish Bioindustry Association, www.ibec.ie/sectors/IBIA/
webIBIA.nsf

Japan Bioindustry Association, www.jba.or.jp
Kentucky Life Sciences Organization, www.klso.com
Los Alamos National Labs, www.lanl.gov/worldview
Maryland Bioscience Alliance, www.mdhitech.org
Massachusetts Biotechnology Council, www.massbio.org
MdBio, Inc., www.mdbio.org
Michigan Biotechnology Association (MichBio),
    www.michbio.org
Minnesota Bio (MNBIO), www.mnbio.org
Missouri Biotechnology Association (MOBIO),
    www.mobio.org
National Academies of Science,
    www.nationalacademies.org
National Academies Library of International Activities,
    www.nas.edu/gateway/international
National Agricultural Biotechnology Council,
    www.nabc.cals.cornell.edu
National Center for Biotechnology Information (NCBI),
    www.ncbi.nlm.nih.gov
National Institute of Standards & Technology (NIST),
    www.nist.gov
New Hampshire Biotechnology Council,
    www.nhbiotech.com
New York Biotechnology Association, www.nyba.org
New York Center for Biotechnology,
    www.biotech.suny.edu
New Zealand Biotechnology Association, www.nzbio.org
Niaba (Netherlands' Biotechnology Association),
    www.niaba.nl

North Carolina Biosciences Organization (NCBIO),
www.ncbioscience.org

North Carolina Biotechnology Center, www.ncbiotech.org

North Carolina Genomics and Bioinformatics
Consortium, LLC, www.ncbiotech.org

North Dakota Agriculture Association, www.ndag.org

Northern California Biotechnology Center, www.ccfs.edu

Northwestern University Center for Biotechnology,
www.kellogg.northwestern.edu/biotech

NRC Biotechnology Research Institute (Canada),
www.bri.nrc-cnrc.ca

NZ Bio, www.nzbio.org

Oklahoma EPSCoR Biotechnology Network,
www.ptf.okstate.edu/epscor

Oregon Bioscience Association, www.oregonbio.org

Ottawa Life Sciences Council, www.olsc.ca

Pennsylvania Biotechnology Association,
www.pennsylvaniabio.org

Pennsylvania Life Sciences Greenhouse, www.lsgpa.com

Peptide & Protein Science Group (United Kingdom),
www.ppsg.org.uk

Pharmaceutical Research & Manufacturers of America,
www.phrma.org

Plant Biotechnology Institute (Canada), www.pbi-ibp.nrc-
cnrc.gc.ca

Quebec Biotechnology Innovation Centre,
www.innovation.gc.ca

Rensselaer Polytechnic Institute, Center for Biotechnology,
www.rpi.edu/research/biotech

Rhode Island Science and Technology Council,
www.stac.ri.gov

San Diego Biocommerce Online, www.biocom.org

Slater Center for Biomedical Technology (Rhode Island),
www.slaterfund.com

Society of Biophysicists of Latin America,
www.biophysics.org

South Carolina Biotechnology Association, www.scbio.org

Southern California Biomedical Council (SCBC),
www.socalbio.org

Spanish Society on Biotechnology, www.sebiot.crib.uam.es

Swiss Biotech Association, www.swissbiotechassociation.ch

Technology Council of Maryland, www.mdhitech.org

Tennessee Biotechnology Association, www.tribio.org

Texas Healthcare & Bioscience Institute, www.thbi.org

Toronto Biotechnology Initiative, www.torontobiotech.org

U.S. National Agricultural Library, www.nal.usda.gov

University of Maryland Biotechnology Institute,
www.umbi.umd.edu

University of Wisconsin Biotechnology Center,
www.biotech.wisc.edu

USDA Agricultural Biotechnology,
www.usda.gov/agencies/biotech

USEPA Environmental Protection Agency, www.epa.gov

USFDA Food and Drug Administration, www.fda.gov

Utah Life Science Association, www.edcutah.org

Virginia Biotechnology Association, www.vabio.org

Washington Biotechnology and Biomedical Association,
www.wabio.com

West Virginia High Technology Consortium Foundation,
www.wvhtf.org

Wisconsin Biotechnology Association,
www.wisconsinbiotech.org

Wyoming Agricultural Business Association,
www.wyag.net

Appendix C

Informatics and Information Sciences Associations

American Medical Informatics Association (AIMA),
www.amia.org

American National Standards Institute (ANSI),
www.ansi.org

American Society for Information Science and Technology
(ASIST), www.asis.org

Association for Applied Interactive Multimedia (AAIM),
www.aaim.org

Association for Information and Image Management
(AIIM), www.aiim.org

Association of College and Research Libraries (ACRL),
www.acrl.org

Canadian Association of Research Libraries, www.carl-
abrc.ca

China Society for Scientific and Technical Information
(CSSTI) (in Chinese and English, first and largest
Chinese research information organization),
www.cssti.org.cn/english

International Association of Technological University
Libraries (IATUL) holds annual international
conference, www.iatul.org

International Medical Informatics Societies (EMIS),
www.emis.org

International Organization for Standardization (ISO)
(largest organization for technical standards, responsible
for ISO 9000 and other quality control standards
systems), www.iso.org

International Society for Knowledge Organization (ISKO),
www.isko.org

Selected Colleges and Universities with Biotechnology or Interdisciplinary Programs

New programs emphasizing biology, biochemistry, and genetics, as well as interdisciplinary biotechnology programs are being added at a rapid rate in colleges and universities in the United States, Canada, Mexico, and many other countries. In addition to the colleges and universities listed here, there are many more excellent schools with biology, chemistry, agricultural, and related majors that provide education and skills that are fundamental to a profession in biotechnology.

Many additional schools may also have biotechnology programs and/or majors at the undergraduate and graduate levels available soon. If you are interested in a particular school, you should check with the admissions department, as well as the subject area department, and request the most complete and up-to-date information available.

Brigham Young University
Provo, UT 84602
www.byu.edu

Boston University School of Medicine
Boston, MA 02118
www.bumc.bu.edu

Cabrini College
Radnor, PA 19087
www.cabrini.edu

California State Polytechnic University
Pomona, CA 91768
www.csupomona.edu

California State University
San Marcos, CA 92096
www.csusm.edu

Calvin College
Grand Rapids, MI 49546
www.calvin.edu

CUNY–York College
Jamaica, NY 11451
www.natlsci.york.cuny.edu

Dalhousie University
Department of Oceanography
Halifax, NS, B3H 4H6
Canada
www.dal.ca

East Stroudsburg University of Pennsylvania
East Stroudsburg, PA 18301-2999
www.3.esu.edu

Elizabethtown College
Biological Sciences
Elizabethtown, PA 17022
www.etown.edu

Fayetteville State University
University of North Carolina
Fayetteville, NC 28301
www.uncfsu.edu

Ferris State University
Biopharmaceutical
Big Rapids, MI 49307
www.ferris.edu

Florida Gulf Coast University
Ft. Myers, FL 33965
www.fgcu.edu

Harvard University
Cambridge, MA 02138
www.fas.harvard.edu

Heidelberg College
Biological Sciences
Tiffin, OH 44883
www.heidelberg.edu

Illinois Institute of Technology (IIT)
Computer Technology
Chicago, IL 60616
www.iit.edu

Indiana University
Biology Department
1001 E. Third St.
Bloomington, IN 47405-3700
www.bio.indiana.edu

James Madison University
Harrisonburg, VA 22807
www.jmu.edu

Kennesaw State University
Kennesaw, GA 30144
http://science.kennesaw.edu

Kent State University
Kent, OH 44242
www.kent.edu

Madison Area Technical College
Madison, WI 53704
www.tec.wi.us

Massachusetts Institute of Technology (MIT)
Cambridge, MA 02139-4307
http://web.mit.edu

McGill University
Montreal, QC, H3A 2T5
Canada
www.mcgill.ca

Miami University
Micro and Molecular Biology, Biosciences
Oxford, OH 45056
www.muohio.edu

Missouri Baptist University
St. Louis, MO 63141-8698
www.mobap.edu

Montana State University
Biochemistry and Biomedical Departments
Bozeman, MT 59717
www.montana.edu

Montgomery College
Biomedical and Biotechnical
Rockville, MD 20850
www.montgomerycollege.edu

North Dakota State University
Fargo, ND 58105
www.ndsu.edu

Northwestern University
Center for Biotechnology
Evanston, IL 60201
www.northwestern.edu

Oak Ridge Associated Universities
Institute for Sciences
P.O. Box 117
Oak Ridge, TN 37831-0117
www.orau.org

Ohio State University
College of Medical and Public Health, Biological Sciences, and
    Pharmacy
Enarson Hall
Columbus, OH 43210
www.osu.edu

Oregon State University
Corvalis, OR 97331-2106
www.oregonstate.edu

Pennsylvania State University
University Park
Eberly College of Science
College Park, PA 16802
www.psu.edu

Plymouth State University
Plymouth, NH 03264-1595
www.oz.plymouth.edu

Point Park University
201 Wood St.
Pittsburgh, PA 15222
www.pointpark.edu

Princeton University
Molecular Biology Dept.
P.O. Box 430
Princeton, NJ 08544-0430
www.princeton.edu

Purdue University
575 Stadium Mall Dr.
West Lafayette, IN 47907
www.mcmp.purdue.edu

Rensselaer Polytechnic Institute
110 8th St.
Troy, NY 12108
www.rpi.edu

Rice University
Bioengineering, Chemical and Biomolecular Engineering
Houston, TX 77005
www.rice.edu

Rochester Institute of Technology
Rochester, NY 14623
www.rit.edu

Roosevelt University
430 S. Michigan Ave.
Chicago, 60605
www.roosevelt.edu

Rutgers–New Brunswick
The State University
Piscataway, NJ 08854-8097
www.rutgers.edu

Salem International University
Biological Sciences Dept.
Salem, WV 26426-0500
www.salemiu.edu

Southeastern Oklahoma State University
Health Technology
PMB 4225
Durant, OK 74701-0609
www.sosu.edu

Southwest Minnesota State University
Marshall, MN 56258
www.southwest.msus.edu

Stanford University
Stanford, CA 94305-3005
www.stanford.edu

SUNY–Upstate Medical University
Biomedical Research
Syracuse, NY 13210-2375
www.upstate.edu

Texas A & M University
Biological Sciences
College Station, TX 77843-1265
www.tamu.edu

University of Arizona
Tucson, AZ 85721-0040
www.arizona.edu

University of British Columbia
Applied Science (including Chemical and Biological Engineering),
   Medicine, Pharmaceutical Sciences
Vancouver, BC V6T 1Z2
Canada
www.ubc.ca
and
Calgary, AB T2N 1N4
Canada
www.ucalgary.ca

University at Buffalo–SUNY
School of Medicine and Biomedical Sciences
Buffalo, NY 14260-1600
www.buffalo.edu

University of California
Applied Science and Technology, Biological Sciences,
   Bioengineering
Berkeley, CA, 94720
www.berkeley.edu

University of California
Davis, CA 95616-8687
www.ucdavis.edu

University of California
Life Sciences Division
Murphy Hall
Los Angeles, CA 90095-1436
www.ucla.edu

University of Cambridge
Departments of Chemistry, Pharmacology, Physics, Statistics,
    Zoology
Cambridge, UK
www.cam.ac.uk/cambuniv

University of Colorado
Colorado Institute of Research in Biotechnology
Fort Collins, CO 80523-1801
www.natsci.colostate.edu

University of Georgia
Georgia Biotechnology Center
Biological Sciences Division
Athens, GA 30602
www.uga.edu

University of Hong Kong
Department of Biology and Science
Pok Fu Lam Road
China
www.hku.hk

University of Houston
1 Main St., Ste. N-813
Houston, TX 77002
www.uhd.edu

University of Illinois
Dept. of Biological Sciences
Banner Dept. 2-453000
3262 SES MC 066
845 W. Taylor
Chicago, IL 60607-7060
www.uic.edu

University of Illinois
College of Medicine
808 S. Wood St. MC-783
Chicago, IL 60612-7302
www.edu.depts/mcam

University of Illinois
Biotechnology Center
Urbana-Champaign, IL 61820
www.biotec.uiuc.edu

University of Kentucky
Health Sciences, Medicine, Pharmacology
Lexington, KY 40506
www.uky.edu

University of Maryland, Baltimore County
Biochemical Engineering, Applied Molecular Biology, Human
    Context of Science and Technology
1000 Hilltop Circle
Baltimore, MD 21250
www.umbc.edu

University of Maryland Biotechnology Institute
Human Health, Marine Environment, Agriculture, Protein Dept.
Rockville, MD 20850
www.umbi.umd.edu

University of Michigan
Life Sciences
Ann Arbor, MI 48109-1002
www.umich.edu

University of Minnesota
College of Biological Sciences
Biotechnology Institute
St. Paul, MN 555108
www.umn.edu

University of Missouri
Biochemistry, Biotechnology, Neurodynamics
1 University Blvd.
St. Louis, MO 63121-4400
www.umsi.edu

University of Montreal
C.P. 6128
Montreal, QC H3C 3J7
Canada
www.umontreal.ca

University of Nebraska
Omaha, NE 68182
www.unomaha.edu

University of Nevada
Mail Stop 120
Reno, NV 89557
www.unr.edu

University of North Carolina
Chapel Hill, NC 27599-3360
www.ils.unc.edu

University of Northern Iowa
Cedar Falls, IA 50613
www.uni.edu

University of Pennsylvania
School of Medicine
Philadelphia, PA 19104-6055
www.med.upenn.edu

University of Rochester Medical Center
Rochester, NY 14627
www.urmc.rochester.edu

University of Tennessee
Knoxville, TN 37996-0220
www.utk.edu

University of Texas–Dallas
School of Engineering and Computer Science, Micro/Nano Devices
   & Systems Laboratory
Richardson, TX 75083-0688
www.utdallas.edu

University of Toronto
Environmental Studies, Computer Science
Toronto, ON M5S 1A3
Canada
www.utoronto.ca

University of Washington
Biomedical, Biochemistry, Biomolecular and Genetics,
    Environmental, Biostatistics, Ocean & Fisheries Sciences
320 Schmitz
Box 355840
Seattle, WA 98185-5840
www.washington.edu

University of Wisconsin
Genetics and Biotechnology Center; DNA Sequencing and
    Synthesis, Gene Expression, Mass Spectrometry, Molecular
    Interaction, Transgenic Facilities
425 Henry Mall
Madison, WI 53706
www.biotech.wisc.edu

University of Wisconsin
College of Agriculture, Food, Environmental Sciences
River Falls, WI 54022-5001
www.uwrf.edu

Virginia Polytechnic Institute and State University
Fralin Biotechnology Center
Blacksburg, VA 24061
www.biotech.vt.edu

Washington State University
Pullman, WA 99164-4660
www.molecular.biosciences.wsu.edu

William Paterson University of New Jersey
Biopsychology, Life Science and Environmental Ethics Honors
   Programs
Wayne, NJ 07470
www.wpunj.edu

Winston-Salem State University
Winston-Salem, NC 27110
www.wssu.edu

Worcester Polytechnic Institute
WPI Life Sciences & Biology Center; Biology, Biotechnology,
   Biochemistry, Biomedical Engineering; Human Limb
   Regeneration Research
100 Institute Rd.
Worcester, MA 01609-2280
www.wpi.edu

Yale University
Molecular, Cellular & Developmental Biology
P.O. Box 208103
New Haven, CT 06520-8103
www.yale.edu

Appendix E

Annotated Bibliography of Selected Journals in Biotechnology and Related Fields

THE PROFESSIONAL JOURNALS described here are published in various countries by universities, research organizations, professional organizations, or publishers. Where needed, the country of publication is also listed. The journals are provided in electronic and/or print editions, and websites are provided for all, where additional details are available.

AgBioForum. Provides broad-based information and innovative ideas in science, public policy, and private strategies related to agricultural biotechnology; United States; www.agbioforum.org

AGBiotech Reporter. Internet website providing news about agricultural biotechnology worldwide, including new products, agricultural biotechnology patents, pharmaceutical biotechnology, and others; United States; www.agra-net.com

Asia Pacific Biotech News. A report on pharmaceuticals, health care, food, and agriculture in the Asia-Pacific region read by health care professionals, investors, academics, and researchers in both Asia-Pacific and the worldwide markets; Singapore, Senegal; http://helecon3.hkkk.fi/journals

BioLink. Provides an e-mail newsletter and back editions of *BioLink*, published by the Special Interest Group on Text Mining (BioLINK); international; www.pdg.chb.uam.es/BioLink

Biomx—Biotechnology Information for the Science Community. Industry and research news, articles, events calendar; includes recommended publications and jobs/career information; United States; www.biomx.org

Biotechnology Advances. Website covers broad areas of biotechnology as well as relevant aspects of biology, chemistry, and engineering; United States; www.elsevier.com/locate/biotech

Biotechnology & Bioengineering. Articles and reviews on applied biotechnology, including cellular physiology; United States; www.3.interscience.wiley.com

Biotechnology Journals. Provides links to a list of bioscience and medical journal homepages; Austria; www.medbioworld.com

Biotechnology Progress. Research reports and reviews of techniques for development and design of new processes and products in the biotechnology and bioprocess industries; United States; www.aiche.org/publications/biotech

Biotechnology Techniques. Covers new techniques in experimental biotechnology; United States; w.ingentaconnect.com/content

BioWorld Switzerland. Website provides news of biotechnology research and industries of Switzerland; in English and German; Switzerland; www.bioworld.ch

Current Advances in Applied Microbiology & Biotechnology. Monthly search service of literature in the field; France; www.medbioworld.com/bio/journals

Current Opinion in Biotechnology; Cell Biology; Chemical Biology; Genetics and Development; Immunobiology; Microbiology; Neurology; Pharmacology; Plant Biology; Structural Biology. Journals of expert review, citing the best publications in each field over the past months, with search service for current and back issues; United States; www.current-opinion.com

DNA Sequence. Journal of mapping data, full DNA sequence data, new sequencing and analysis procedures, and related techniques; United Kingdom; www.tandf.co.uk.journals

Electronic Journal of Biotechnology. International UNESCO e-journal that publishes papers from broad range of areas that are related to biotechnology; Chile; www.ejbiotechnology .info

Gene. International journal on genes, genomes, and evolution; Netherlands; www.elseviere.com/locate/journals

Gene Function & Disease. Wiley-VCH publication of clinically important basic research in molecular biology; United States; www.3interscience.wiley.com

Gene Sciences & DNA Jobs. Information about biotechnology jobs and résumés; United States; www.genesciences.com

Genetic Engineering News (GEN). Industrial biotechnology, biopharmaceutical, agricultural, chemical, enzyme, and environmental news, from research projects through commercialization; United States; www.genengnews.com

Genome Research. Genome research and genome-based analyses of human and other animal biological processes; United States; www.genome.org

GenomeWeb. Provides print and electronic publications of global news and information on agricultural genomics business and technology, and bioinformatics; United States; www.genomeweb.com

Journal of Bioscience and Bioengineering. Information about fermentation technology, biochemical engineering, food technology, and microbiology; Netherlands; www.elsevier.locate/jfermbio

Journal of Chemical Technology and Biotechnology. Journal covering fields of chemical technology and biotechnology, especially where the fields interact; United States; www.3.interscience .wiley.com

Journal of Microbiology & Biotechnology. Official publication of the Korean Society for Applied Microbiology; covering topics in biotechnology and microbiology; Korea; http://www.bric .postech.ac.kr

Mammalian Genome. Experimental and technical aspects of genomics and genetics in human and other mammals in gene function studies; Netherlands; www.springer.com/journal

Molecular Engineering. Journal dealing with studies of design, characterization, and application of molecules and molecular materials and their specific biological, chemical, and physical properties; Netherlands; www.kluweronline.com

Nature Biotechnology. Biological research papers with potential for commercial agricultural, environmental, medical, and pharmaceutical development; job listings; United States; www.nature.com

Nucleic Acids Research. Monthly journal of scientific, research, and database topics; United States; www.nar.oxfordjournals.org

Protein Expression and Purification. A forum for information about protein isolation based on fractionation and techniques using molecular biological procedures to increase protein expression; United States; www.elsevier.com/locate/yprep

Reviews in Molecular Biotechnology. Scientific reviews of current biomolecular technologies and new technologies becoming available in the near future; United States; www.humana press.com

World Journal of Microbiology and Biotechnology. Provides forum for research on microbiological and biotechnological solutions for major global problems; United States; www.com/site/catalog/journal

About the Author

Sheldon S. Brown is a well-known writer/photographer and journalist who has written about science and scientific topics for many years. His illustrated articles have appeared in a number of general interest magazines such as *Collector's World, Ford Times, Parade, Popular Photography, The Rotarian,* and *Science Digest.* He is also known for his many contributions to specialized publications in the business field.

Brown is the author of three previous books. He has been listed in *Contemporary Authors, Contemporary Journalists, The International Authors and Writers Who's Who, Michigan Authors and Poets, Who's Who in the Midwest,* and *The Working Press of the Nation.*